SILVIO L

Controlled Trading

10 laws

to control the market

Copyright © 2019 Silvio Luppi

All rights reserved, and any unauthorized reproduction, even partial, is prohibited.

The trademark "Controlled Trading" is personal property.

For any information, explanations and inquiries for the use of this work in contexts different from private reading please contact:

tradingcontrollato@gmail.com

Contents

Introduction--pag. 5

Chap.1 Basic technical analysis---------------------------------pag. 7

Chap.2 Psychology in technical analysis----------------------pag. 56

Chap.3 10 laws to control the market----------------------------pag. 64

Chap.4 Trading Marketing--pag. 137

Chap.5 Real cases--pag. 144

References--pag. 156

Foreword

Over the last few years the online trading world has seen significant changes, and I don't mean in terms of markets, but in terms of marketing policies used by the various brokers which have led many people, eager to change their lifestyle, to jump on the band wagon thinking they could easily earn money at home by simply clicking a couple of well thought out mouse clicks... Unfortunately, this is not the case! Trading requires a lot of study, time, commitment, discipline and plenty of dedication. Then, the best trader can achieve the myth of profit-making clicks on the Polynesian coast.

Introduction

I decided to write this book, which can be considered as a set of rules, because my goal is to lead the trader beyond that boundary that divides those who earn money from those who lose money within the financial markets.

I don't want to repeat the old story that I heard a thousand times - 90% of those who operate on the stock exchange lose money etc. instead, I want to show you what are the techniques that really make the difference between earning and losing money. So you can join that famous 10% that all traders desire.

This book is divided into two sections:

-A first part aimed at those who are eager to start a learning path, in fact in the relative chapters I also recommend books, manuals, sites and youtube channels to visit and study in order to receive a training as rich and complete as possible.

-The second part on the other hand, is aimed at those who already do online trading, those who make use of technical analysis, and those who lose money and control in front of their monitor, maybe for not having closed the position sooner or for not letting it run when it was profitable.

I wrote this book because it is the book that I would have loved to have when I started trading with poor results. In fact, despite having studied lots of volumes on technical analysis as never before to get positive results,

I could not earn money, lost money... THAT WAS CRAZY... I studied, spent time, effort and then I also lost money...

Do you see yourself in this example?

Well, this book aims at discoling those secrets, which are not really secrets, but if no one tells you they remain unrevealed. This will help you to always have control of the market and become a successful trader.

Chapter 1

Basic technical analysis

This chapter is for those who have discovered this book without having any previous knowledge of technical analysis. Whether you have bought it, found it or picked it up from the basket, I have the duty to give - at least - the basic information to help you understand what I wrote.

All readers who are already familiar with the basics of trading can skip straight to chapter two, although a refresher won't hurt.

1.1 Types of analysis

There are two methods used by traders to enter different markets on the stock exchange, which are:

- Fundamental analysis:
  It tries to determine the value of a financial instrument by analyzing everything. For example it analyzes a company's balance sheet if you trade in stocks, or it forecasts about the interest rate if you trade currencies. All this is done to understand whether a particular financial instrument is over or under estimated. It is important to underline that news do not so much move the markets per se, but the reactions of traders to such news.
- Technical analysis:
  It studies the market movement through the systematic use of

charts to predict future price trends. This book is totally dedicated to this.

1.2 Financial instruments

For a technical approach the financial instruments available on the various online platforms, are:

- Commodities: Oil, gold, silver, natural gas, wheat, cotton, coffee, etc. are part of this group.
- Indexes: These are pools of stocks that represent the average stock performance giving greater weight to those with greater capitalization and vice versa. The main indexes are the FTSMIB, DAX 30, Nasdaq, etc.
- Forex: This category includes all currency exchange rates, e.g. EUR/GBP, EUR/USD, USD/CAD, EUR/JPY, etc.
- Stocks: Financial instrument that represents the minimum fraction of participation in the share capital of a company. Thanks to online platforms it is now possible to exchange shares of the world's major companies, such as Apple, Amazon, Mc. Donalds, Deutche Bank, Telecom Italia etc.
- Options: These are derivative financial instruments, which give the owner the right to buy or sell a specific underlying asset at a fixed price within the expiration of the option itself. Options are therefore associated with underlying assets, for example shares or indexes, which determine their price.

- Criptocurrency: These are all the virtual coins that provide safe and autonomous operations. They became part of the financial instruments a few years ago, and are very volatile. The main ones are: Bitcoin, Ripple, Litecoin and Ethereum.

Technical analysis provides operators the possibility to analyse all these financial instruments, but the most reliable ones are: forex, commodities and indexes. As far as stocks are concerned, it is worth pointing out that this market is easier to manipulate, as it is much more difficult for operators to know different inter-company dynamics, therefore even a specific graphic analysis could lead to not obtaining the expected profits.

1.3 Charts

Before showing you the cases I would like to clarify a few things for a better reading of the charts:

- All the images are from my personal profile on the Tradingview.com platform.

- I chose to use the colour black and white to make it easier for the reader to understand these charts. Of course, within the Tradingview.com platform you can freely select the colours you like.

- White-body and black-edged candlesticks are the bullish ones.

- Black-body and white-edged candlesticks are the bearish ones

- The black lines on the graph represent static and dynamic supports and resistances.

- As I searched for the best charts of analysis and past operations. As a result, the price at the time of the screenshot, besides being useless, would just cause a lot of confusion.

Throughout the years in the field of technical analysis many types of charts have been created, all with different characteristics, The two most famous and most used charts by operators are:

> Linear chart: This type of chart is the easiest to draw, in fact it only examines the closing price of the financial tool taken into consideration. Its main purpose is to provide the primary direction of prices.

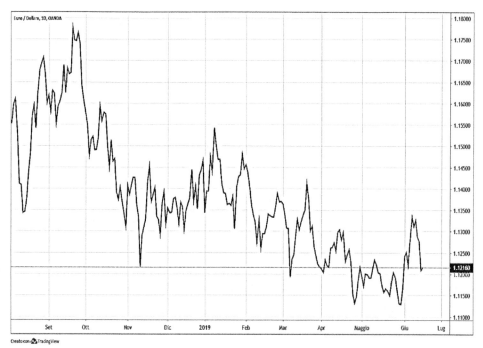

Image 1.1: Linear chart

The above image is an example of a linear chart. As you can read at the top left we are on the euro/dollar exchange rate on the 24 hour time frame. The pitcture you see highlighted on the right of the chart (1.12160) is the value of the exchange rate when I took the screenshot from my computer.

> Candlestick: This type of chart is among the most used, due to the completeness offered by the Japanese candlesticks.

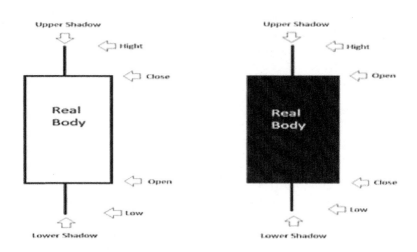

Image 1.2: Japanese candlesticks

As you can see in the image above the candlesticks are composed of two elements: a central body called real-body, which represents the distance between the opening and the closing price (this will be white if the session was positive or black if it was negative); and two shadows which are thin lines representing the maximum price (upper shadow) and the minimum price (lower shadow) reported during the session. Using the candlestick chart you can easily find signals of continuation or reversal of the trend, which is why many traders study the markets with this type of chart.

Image 1.3: Candlestick chart

The above chart is an example of a candlestick chart of the New Zealand euro/dollar exchange rate on a 24 hour time frame. A 24 hours' time frame means that each candlestick represents a trading day. The trader can freely define the time frame, which can most commonly range between one-hour, 4-hour, daily and weekly. The figure shown on the right of the chart, 1.67583, is the value of the exchange rate at the time I took the screenshot. This type of chart allows traders to understand not only the market value, like the linear chart, but also the price behaviour recorded during the whole trading session.

1.4 What is a trend?

By trend we mean the movement of the market, which can be of three types:

-**Bullish:** when prices move upwards, i.e. over time they are raising highs and lows.

Image 1.4: Bullish trend

- **Bearish:** when prices show a downward movement, i.e. over time they show lower highs and lower lows.

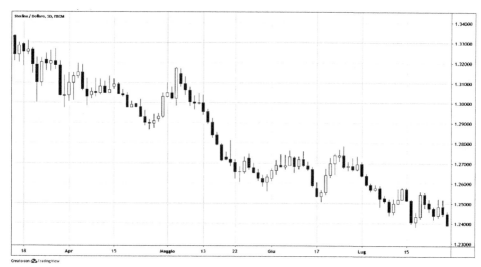

Image 1.5: Bearish trend

- **Sideways:** when prices move within a well-defined range, i.e. prices over time always swing between the same values without showing a variation of either highs or lows.

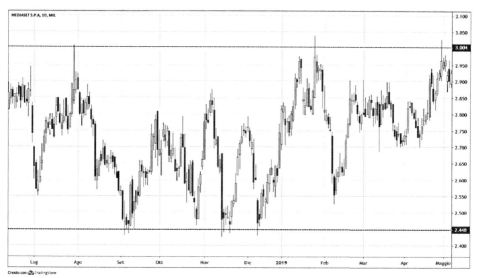

Image 1.6: Sideways trend

The objective of the analyst is to find the main trend and follow it until it shows evident signs of inversion, in fact it is more likely that a trend has a continuous trend rather than an unexpected inversion. This consideration originates one of the most important sentences of the whole technical analysis: **THE TREND IS YOUR FRIEND.**

In regards to trading on the stock exchange there are two types of operations that an analyst can do: they are called long when the trader buys a financial instrument and will try to sell it once it has a higher price in the market; short when the trader sells a financial instrument without owning it and later, will try to buy it at a lower price to make a profit. Essentially, the trader will open long positions when he believes that prices can go up and short positions when he believes that prices will go down.

1.5 Stop loss & take profit

Every analyst who works in the financial markets must always consider, before opening a position, how much he or she is willing to lose if the investment is wrong, and how much they could potentially profit. This is why in every operation it is important to set the stop loss and take profit.

Stopping a loss means setting a limit to the losses of a wrong investment. Should the threshold be hit by the prices the position would be closed immediately and automatically, also it is essential to keep in mind some criteria when setting it.

First of all the stop loss must be sustainable, therefore it must not significantly affect the capital of the trader, e.g. if an investor has a total capital of 1000 euros he cannot afford to place a stop loss with a potential loss of 600 euros, because if it is affected by prices his capital would be significantly impacted.

Secondly, stop losses must be well set, following the main rules of technical analysis.

Thirdly, once the stop loss is placed by the trader, it must never be moved or even removed, as it could have catastrophic consequences for the available capital. Finally the stop to the losses must always be placed on a financial tool, because the market at any time could make sudden and unpredictable movements that could lead to huge losses.

By taking profit we mean to set a limit to the potential profits, since just like in the stop loss, once it is hit by the prices of the set value the position is immediately closed. Also in this case it is very important that the take profit is always properly set and that it is never removed or moved. Even if, at first, the take profit does not seem to be very important, it becomes key when a trader has to plan his investments, therefore he should try to predict in advance how much a certain position will benefit him.

1.6 Support & resistance

Support and resistance are price levels that form a balance between the strength of supply and that of the demand, the formation of these becomes therefore an excellent chance for traders to understand the market trend and be able to profit from it. The support and resistance can be both static and dynamic, for the latter the most appropriate term is trend-line. From a graphical point of view they are straight lines that combine several price levels which are drawn by the analyst with the function of making market movements easier. To best explain every single situation and understand how to take action when you are on one of them it is better to make a case by case distinction:

- Static support: It usually occurs within a bearish trend or within a sideways period, it is a price level in which the interest of buyers becomes strong enough to overcome the pressure of sellers, the consequence will be a stop of the bearish trend and an increase in prices.

Image 1.7: Static support

The chart above is an indication of the Intesa San Paolo stock, as you can see the prices have touched several times, 5 to be exact, the support (the horizontal straight line that I drew at the level of 1.8065) and then from there they are spread upwards. I would like to point out that prices do not always bounce back from the support, sometimes they actually break through it, which is a strong sign of the continuation of the bearish trend. Always taking as example the Intesa San Paolo diagram, if the prices had gone down under the level of 1.8065 it would have been a sign of the bearish trend's strength.

- Static resistance: It usually occurs within a bullish trend or within a sideways phase, it is a price level where the interest of sellers becomes strong enough to overcome buyers' pressure, the consequence will be a halt of the rise and a reduction in prices.

Figure 1.8: Static resistance

The above graph is an indication of the American index S&P500, as you can see the prices reach twice the resistance (the horizontal line I drew at the level of 2940) and then, they move downwards. As in the case of the static support, the prices don't always bounce back from the resistance, they sometimes break through it. Again, this is a strong indication of the continuation in the bullish trend.

In reference to the same example above, if the prices had risen above the level of 2940.4 it would have been an indication of the bullish trend's strength.

Please remember what has been said about static supports and resistances because the topic will be further discussed in the third law of the third chapter.

- Dynamic support or bullish trend-line: It occurs within a bullish trend and is a very useful tool because it allows the trader to merge through an inclined line, two or more rising lows. This type of trend-line detects increasingly high levels of support, which provide clear operational indicators to the analysts.

Finally, the longer the time, the more contact points there are, thus the stronger and more significant the trend will be.

Image 1.9: Bullish trend-line

The chart above is an example of the candlestick chart of the Euro/Australian dollar exchange rate on a 24 hours' time frame. As you can clearly see from the image the prices have bounced several times back from the bullish trend-line, marking increasing highs and lows over time.

- Dynamic resistance or bearish trend-line: It occurs within a bearish trend and it is a very helpful tool because it allows the trader to merge two or more decreasing highs along a straight inclined line. This type of trend-line finds increasingly low levels of resistance, which provide analysts with clear operational indicators. Finally, just like in the bullish trend-line, the harder it is over time, the more contact points there are, and thus the stronger and more significant the trend will be.

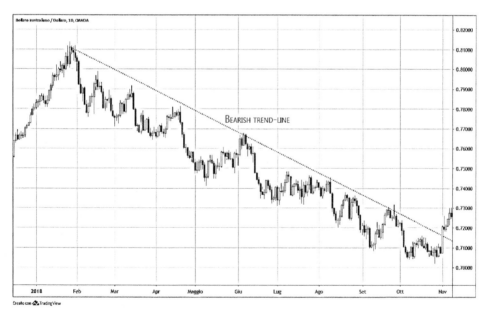

Image 1.10: Bearish trend-line

The chart above is an example of the candlestick chart of the Australian dollar/US dollar exchange rate on a daily time frame. As you can clearly see from the image, prices have bounced several times from the bearish trend-line, hitting descending highs and lows over time. This image is very explanatory as it allows to understand, besides the importance of the trend-line in defining the primary trend, the case in which these are breached. Indeed, the white candle that you see in the bottom right breaches the dynamic resistance and defines the end of the bearish trend and the beginning of a potential bullish trend.

1.7 Breakout

Typically when a static or dynamic support or resistance is broken by prices we are talking about a BREAKOUT. In the chart above, the point in which the white candlestick overcomes the bearish trend-line is called breakout or breaking point.

Let's see in detail some characteristics of breakouts and how to get the most out of them:

- When the breakout occurs, of both static and dynamic support, you have a very strong operating signal and a trader should use it to open a short position, placing the stop loss above the support. This because the breakout confirms that the balance between buyers and sellers has broken, and the latter have gained control of the market.

- When a breakout of both static and dynamic resistance takes place, there is a clear operational signal and a trader should use it to open upward positions, placing the stop loss below the resistance. This is because, as in the previous case, the breakout shows that the balance between buyers and sellers has broken, and the former has taken over.

- Thirdly, it is important to emphasize that when a static resistance is broken upwards it becomes an important price level and turns into a static support. Vice versa will happen if a breakout occurs to decrease of a support.

- A "retest" on the support or on the resistance is defined as the moment when prices, once a resistance or support is broken, make a correction and return to hit what has become the new support or resistance (as in point 3 of the chart below). It is definitely the best moment in which a trader can position himself in the market, indeed, at that very moment you have the best risk/return ratio. Taking the chart below as an example, the best trade is to enter *long* once the prices have gone to retest the resistance they previously broke (the new support) placing the stop loss below the support itself.

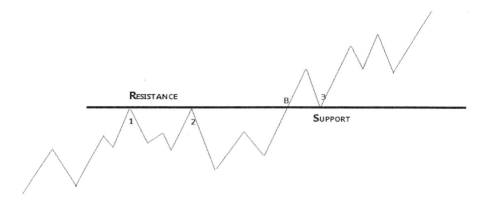

Image 1.11: Retest after the breakout of a static resistance

- The retest happens very often even after a trend-line breakout. In this case the prices, once a trend line is broken to rise or to fall, they tend to hit it one last time before proceeding in the direction of the breakout (point 4 of the image below). As in the case of supports and static resistances it represents the best moment to enter the market with excellent risk/return ratios.

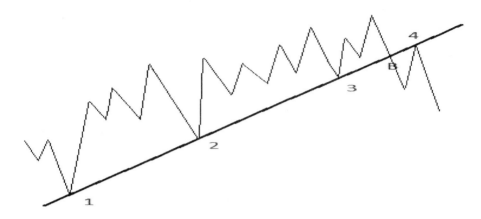

Image 1.12: Retest after a breakout in a bullish trend line

- The support and resistance retest does not always take place, so the trader who waits for the retest for the best risk/return ratio cannot always enter the position. Personally, I prefer and advise to wait for it, in order to avoid excessive stop losses, as when supports and resistances are broken they usually do so in high volumes.
- It is essential when working with supports and resistances to wait until the end of the day to have the confirmation of the breakout, in fact it may happen that the shade of a candlestick exceeds the support, but not the body of it. In this case the trader does not have to operate because the chart is telling us that for a moment the sellers have taken over, but the situation is back in balance at the end of the day, so there are no certain signals. The same applies in case you are in the presence of primary and secondary resistances.

1.8 Candlestick analysis

The candlestick analysis is one of the most important and most used graphic types for the analysis of financial markets, especially for swing trading and day trading, because it provides important operating indications, hard to find in other graphic types. The main aspect of Japanese candles is that they offer an immediate understanding of the psychological dynamics that occur in the short term, allowing analysts to study the effects of what happens in the market and not the causes that generated them. In fact the candlestick analysis highlights the interaction between buyers and sellers also providing important operating signals that, if properly exploited, can lead to important gains. There are numerous types of candles, below I will describe only the main ones:

> Standard line: These are the most classic candles that are most commonly found in the financial markets. This category is sub-divided in turn into long line and short line candles; both can be both positive (white) and negative (black). The long line ones are recognizable because they have a long *real body* and are generally a confirmation of the direction of the main trend as an expression of a movement day. The short line ones introduce a minimal difference between the opening and the closing prices, therefore they have a reduced *real body*, and they are typical candles of indecision. Finally, with regard to all the standard line shadows are not particularly important.

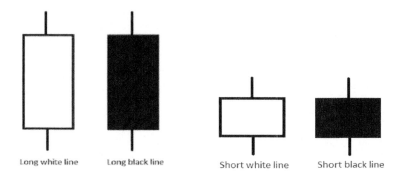

Image 1.13: Long standard line and short standard line

> Spinning top: Are candles that present a relatively small body and long shadows, when they are formed on the markets they show a balance between buyers and sellers, the colour of the body of the candle is not particularly important: Finally it must be emphasized that when they are at the end of a movement phase they assume the name of star, as they contribute to the formation of a sign of inversion.

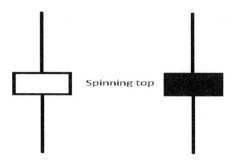

Image 1.14: Spinning top

- ➢ Doji: These candles are formed when the opening price is the same as the closing price, therefore they do not have real body, but only long shadows. When they are created they indicate a phase of uncertainty, but they can also constitute a pause in a marked trend. According to their graphical structure they can be classified in five different categories:
  - o Neutral doji: Candle featuring a very small body and two shadows of modest length. It indicates a phase of indecision with low volatility.
  - o Long-doji: Candle Identical to neutral doji, with the only difference that it has two longer shadows. It indicates a balance between buyers and sellers with high volatility.
  - o Gravestone doji: Candle featuring a correspondence between the opening price, the closing price and the minimum recorded during the day, but with a long upper shadow. When this occurs at the end of a bullish trend it indicates that buyers tried to push the value of the financial tool higher, but were rejected by sellers. The doji gravestone is regarded as a bearish reversal candle and often indicates the presence of resistance.
  - o Dragonfly doji: A candle featuring a correspondence between the opening price, the closing price and the maximum recorded during the day, but with a long lower shadow. When this occurs at the end of a bearish trend it points out that sellers have tried to push the value of the financial tool lower, but have been rejected by buyers.

The dragonfly doji is considered a bullish reversal candle and often indicates the presence of support.

- o Four price doji: A candle that is formed when all four prices, (opening, closing, maximum and minimum) match. It is a combination that is very rarely seen on the financial markets and indicates an absence of volatility and great uncertainty.

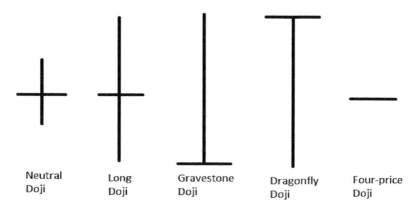

Image 1.15: The five kinds of doji

➢ Hanging man & Hammer: These two candles have the same visual structure that is a real body located only in the upper part of the candle and a long lower shadow. The hanging man and the hammer have different meanings for the operators depending on the colour of the real body and their position within the graph. As far as the first one is concerned, it occurs at the end of a bullish trend, with a black real body, and it provides a signal for inversion, more precisely when it is found it is correct to speak of correction, as it is only a signal of pause in the main trend, therefore for analysts it is appropriate to close any long positions and wait for signals from the market. The hammer on the contrary, is at the end of a bearish trend, it has a white real body and provides a stronger bullish signal of inversion compared to the hanging man. When analysts find this candle in the market it is advisable to wait for confirmation from the next session to try to open upward positions.

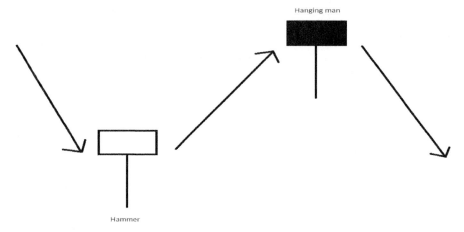

Image 1.16: Hammer & Hanging man

> ➤ Inverted hammer & shooting star: These two candles have the same graphic structure, which is a real body located only in the lower part of the candle and a long upper shadow. The inverted hammer and the shooting star assume, however, different meanings for the operators depending on the colour of the real body and their position within the graph. The former occurs at the end of a bearish trend, with a real body of white colour, and provides a signal of inversion, more precisely when it takes place, it is correct to speak of correction, as it is a signal of only the pause of the main trend, therefore for analysts it is appropriate to close any long positions and wait for further

signals from the market. The latter, on the contrary, is at the end of a bullish trend, it presents a black real body and provides a signal of bullish reversal, stronger if compared to that of the inverted hammer. When analysts find this candle in the market it is appropriate to wait for confirmation from the next session to try to open upward positions.

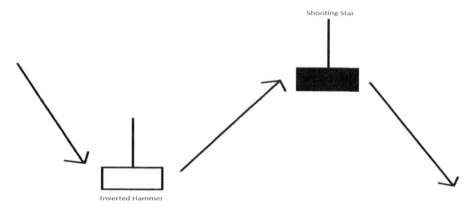

Image 1.17: Inverted hammer & shooting star

So far we have only discussed single candles, but in the trading world there are also combinations of two or more candles that allow traders to understand the market. They are called **Pattern candlestick**.

Here I will describe only the main patterns, for anyone who wants to learn more about Japanese candles, I suggest studying "Candlestick charting explained" by Gregory Morris.

> Engulfing line: It is one of the most important graphical inversion patterns that can be found in the market. It can be either bullish engulfing or bearish engulfing. The two patterns are specular so I will analyse only the bullish engulfing. From the graphic point of view this pattern always forms inside a solid bearish directional movement, at the end of which there is a small black standard line followed by a long white candle that extends entirely above and below the previous one. A final important consideration about the engulfing line is that when it occurs, high volumes are reported, a clear sign that the market sentiment is changing. To make the most of this inversion signal, the trader will have to open an upward position once the day is over, placing the stop loss just below the lowest point recorded by the big white candle. It is worth noting that the melting of candles that form a bullish engulfing creates a hammer, whereas in the bearish formation it creates a shooting star.

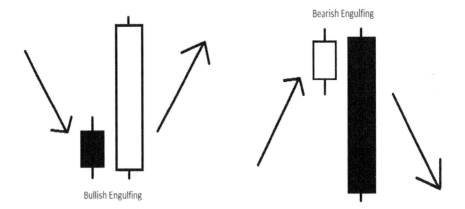

Image 1.18: Bullish engulfing & bearish engulfing

- ➢ Dark-cloud cover & piercing line: These are two highly important inversion patterns and are particularly well known within the technical analysis. The dark cloud cover manifests itself at the end of a bullish trend, therefore it is a bearish reversal signal, while the piercing line appears at the end of a downward movement, and therefore it shows a bullish signal. Below I will analyse only the dark-cloud cover, since the two graphic configurations are specular to each other. From a graphic point of view the dark-cloud cover is made up of two candles with a long real body of opposite colours: the first one will be white and will confirm the current bullish trend; while the second one will be black and will open in *gap-up* (thus above the closing price compared to the previous one) to then close the session with prices that will exceed half of the previous candle. When an analyst finds such a pattern he will be able to open downward positions to take advantage of the trend reversal, placing the stop loss above the opening price of the second candle. Finally it is important to note that the dark-cloud cover and the piercing line are weaker inversion signals compared to the engulfing line, it is therefore advisable to wait for an additional candle to confirm the hypothesis of inversion.

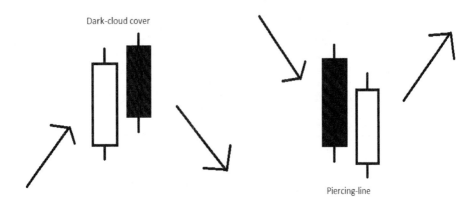

Image 1.19: Dark-cloud cover e Piercing-line

> Morning star & evening star: The morning star and evening star are two inversion patterns that happen at the end of a bearish (morning star) or bullish (evening star) trend; both of the graphic configurations consist of three candles. Below I will analyse only one of the two patterns, since they are specular between them. The morning star provides a sign of bullish reversal at the end of a bearish trend. From a graphical perspective such figure of reversal is characterised by a long black candle, which is coherent with the bearish trend, subsequently a doji or a spinning top appears, which lets understand that within the market it is creating uncertainty, finally a long white candle appears which provides the bullish signal and leads to believe that the feeling of the market has changed. There are two important points to make about the

morning star: the volumes of the first black candle must be lower than those of the last green candle; and the minimum reached by the doji, or the spinning top, must be the minimum touched by the market in all three sessions. From an operating point of view, when a pattern of this type is detected, you can open upward positions without waiting for further signals, positioning the stop loss below the minimum reached by the prices in the formation of the second candle.

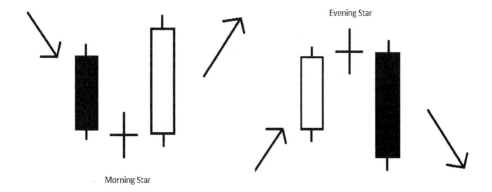

Image 1.20: Morning star & evening star

I would like to highlight that when you find these patterns within a chart it is not mandatory to enter immediately into position, on the contrary you can easily wait to have further confirmation from the market movements and operate only when the yield risk ratio is good enough.

1.9 Patterns

Patterns are shapes that form on the chart due to price movements, as thoroughly illustrated in the book "Technical Analysis of Financial Markets" by John Murphy. These patterns are very important for traders, as they have a predictive value, so they allow them to build operational strategies to take advantage of market movements. These patterns are divided into two macro-categories: continuation and inversion.

Rectangles

The rectangle is a very simple shape to find and shows a breakout in the main trend, where prices start to move sideways. This pattern is characterized by a price swing within two parallel lines, a static support and a dynamic resistance. The shape is defined by volumes surely lower than those in a phase of trend, even if the reduction is less evident than in other shapes.

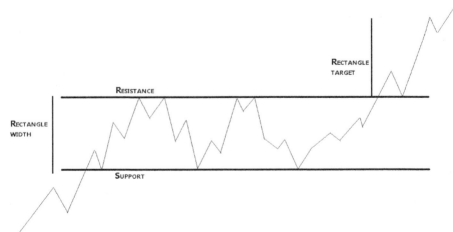

Image 1.21: Rectangle

When you find this kind of shape you can adopt two different strategies:

- The first one is to wait for the exit of the prices from the sideways phase, thus the breakout of either the support or resistance, and then enter the market. When you adopt a strategy of this type it is very important to evaluate the size of the volumes, because if you see that in the rising phase (inside the rectangle) the volumes are greater than in the falling phase, you will have to expect a breakout of the resistance. Vice versa, if the downward movements are greater than the upward ones.
- The second strategy is to take advantage of the sideways phase to open long positions when the price bounces off the support, and to enter the market downwards when the price bounces off the resistance.

A point that can be made on the rectangle by considering its length (temporary duration) and its width (the thickness of the lateral phase) is that the more the wider these variables are, the stronger the movement will be once the rectangle is broken. In support of this thesis there is the demonstration that the target of the figure, the level that the prices would have to reach in the phase after the breakout, will be equal to the width of the rectangle, that is the distance between the support and the resistance.

Triangles

The triangles constitute a pause of the existing trend, they are characterized by the fact that the range in which prices move, consequently the volumes too, tends to decrease as the breakout time approaches. There are three main types of triangle:

- Symmetrical Triangle: The figure is formed inside two trend-lines, one bearish and one bullish, consequently over time we'll witness a gradual increase of the minimums and a reduction of maximums. The possible breakout forecasts should be based on the main trend.
- Ascending Triangle: The figure is formed between a static resistance and a dynamic support, thus over time we will see an increase in the minimums, with the highs remaining unchanged. This price behaviour makes you estimate the greater strength of the buyers compared to the sellers, so you will expect an upward breakout.
- Descending Triangle: This figure is formed between a static support and a dynamic resistance, therefore over time there will be a decrease in the highs, with the lows that will remain unchanged. This price behaviour makes you estimate the greater strength of the sellers compared to the buyers, so you will expect a downward breakout.

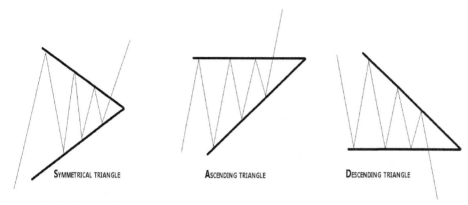

Image 1.22: Types of triangles

When you find these figures it is always better to wait for the support's or resistance's breakout before entering the market, as it is difficult and risky to exploit the sideways as in the case of the rectangle. The target, that is the level that prices should reach once the breakout has occurred, can be established by projecting from the breaking point the base of the triangle, defined as the maximum amplitude that the figure has recorded during its formation.

Head and shoulders

The head and shoulders is one of the most important inversion figures that can occur within the financial markets, it can be both bullish and bearish. In the following I will analyse the bearish head and shoulders, but everything about the latter will be applicable in a specular way to the bullish head and shoulders.

This inversion figure is characterized by some phases:

1. First of all, in order for the formation of a bearish head and shoulders to begin, the market must continue its positive trend characterized by strong volumes as seen in point (a).

2. Subsequently, a correction of the trend along with a reduction in volumes takes place, as shown in point (b). Thanks to the movement, first in (a) then in (b), the left shoulder is formed.

3. Then the bullish trend starts again and reaches point (c), though with smaller volumes. This should be seen as a red flag by analysts, who should sense that the strength of the buyers is reducing.

4. The prices begin to make a new correction up to point (d), this decrease will proceed beyond the peak recorded in (a), coming close to the lowest point (b), and clearly indicate that something is wrong with the bullish trend. Thanks to the movement first in (b) then in (c) and finally in (d) the head is formed.

5. The market goes back up again and reaches point (e), with low volumes, without being able to exceed the previous maximum reached in (c). Once the analyst finds himself in this situation he must close any long positions and wait for prices to give the reversal signal. Thanks to the movement first in (d) then in (e), the right shoulder is formed.

6. Now you can draw a trend-line that crosses points (b) and (d). This will be called neckline and usually has a slight bullish inclination. Only once prices have broken this level will the trader have confirmation that the market has started a bearish trend. Traders will then have to open short positions to take advantage of this movement.

7. Lastly, to calculate the price target you must take the height of the figure (the distance between point (c) and the neckline) and project it downwards from the breakout point.

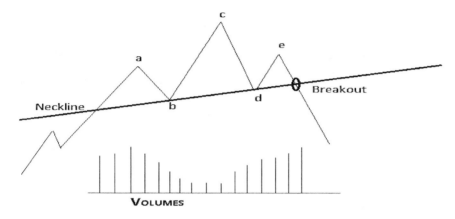

Image 1.23: Bearish head and shoulders

Double top and double bottom

The double top and double bottom are some of the most popular inversion figures in the financial markets. They are comparable to "M" or "W". Below I will analyse the double maximum, but everything concerning the latter will be applicable in a specular way to the double minimum.

When you find a double top it means that the financial tool has reached twice a determined level of price without ever being able to break it, in practice it can be said that it has bounced for a couple of times on a resistance. Subsequently the prices go back down again and exceed the minimum previously created, providing a clear bearish signal. It is worth pointing out that the volumes that are formed in the presence of the second top are lower than those of the first one, this indicates to the operators that the strength of the buyers is weakening, while that of the sellers is intensifying. Additionally, in the descending phase we'll witness to an increase of the volumes, important warning, because it confirms the reversal of the main trend. Finally, to determine the target of this figure it is necessary to project downwards from the breaking point of the figure the distance between one of the two maximum and the intermediate minimum between them.

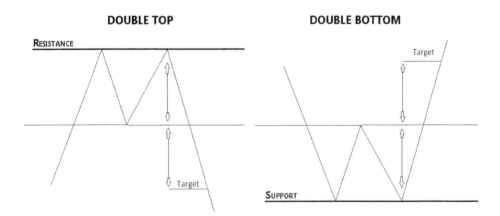

Figure 1.24: Double top and double bottom

There are also the triple top and triple bottom, they have the same structure as the double top and double bottom, but with the only difference that prices bounce three times instead of two on the resistance, in the case of triple top or support in the case of triple bottom. As for the the target, this is calculated like in the previous case.

1.10 Indicators and oscillators

Indicators are fundamental tools for technical analysis, in fact they enable operators to find the main trend followed by prices, to reduce all those information asymmetries coming from the market, moreover they can confirm possible inversion signals and provide relevant information about the main trend. In regard to the oscillators it is important to mention the three main functions they play:

- They identify market situations characterized by an excess of demand (overbought) or supply (oversold). We speak of overbought when the prices cross a bullish directional phase in little time with important volumes, vice versa we will find ourselves in an oversold phase. When the oscillator is in these situations we will have to expect a sideways phase or a possible correction of the prices. It is important to emphasize that when the trend is very well defined, prices may continue to rise even if you are in an overbought or oversold phase.
- Oscillators provide potential buying or selling signals, these operating signals will be different depending on the type of oscillator you decide to use.
- They give information to the operators about the directionality and the strength of the trend, therefore they can identify the moment in which the demand takes over the supply and vice versa, enabling the analysts to detect and therefore anticipate possible reversals of trend. We speak of positive divergence, when the oscillator does

not confirm the negative trend that is crossing the market. In this scenario the chart shows decreasing lows, while the oscillator detects increasing lows, vice versa we are in presence of a negative divergence when the oscillator does not confirm the positive trend of the prices.

Image 1.25: Positive divergence and negative divergence

There are various indicators and oscillators, below I will discuss the main and most used ones, without focusing on the mathematical formulas to get them, since these can be particularly complex, and the technical analysis programs can provide an immediate construction.

Moving averages

Moving averages are undoubtedly the most used and known technical indicators within the whole technical analysis. Their success is due to the fact that they are easy to make, they provide signals of unquestionable interpretation and they can be customized, tested and modified. Moving averages are regarded as the average of a certain amount of data, which can be chosen by traders, indeed there are 10-period, 50-period, and even 200-period averages, the analyst can choose from, based on his experience and his trading method. To calculate an average, you just need to start from the total of the last X prices, for example, for a 20-period average you need to add the last 20 closing prices, and divide them by the number of prices added together. Moving averages are classified into three types:

- Simple moving average: This is calculated as the sum of prices and division of this result by the number of prices added together. The main drawback of this indicator is that when applied to long time series it takes into equal consideration both recent and remote data.
- Weighted moving average: It is calculated with a more complex mathematical formula that allows you to attribute more importance to recent values than to distant ones. Surely, as a moving average it is more precise than the simple one, because it is assumed that the most recent values are able to better interpret what happens on the market.
- Exponential moving average: Very similar to the weighted moving average, other than when applied to very long time series it includes remote values in its calculation, unlike the weighted one.

Moreover, the analyst can personally decide the percentage weight to be attributed to the last closing price that is formed in the market. From an operational perspective, the moving average provides a bullish operational signal when it is cut from the bottom upwards by prices, while it provides a bearish signal when it is cut from the top downwards. It is worth noting that the longer is the period considered calculating the moving average, the stronger and more accurate the signal will be.

Image 1.26: Price intersection with moving average

An advanced method of using this indicator is to use two moving averages on different time frames in order to have a slower and a faster moving average, for example you can use a 50-period average and a 20-period average. The operational signals that are obtained when such a strategy is used are: a bullish signal when the fast moving average cuts up the slow one, and a bearish signal when the fast moving average cuts down the slow one.

Lastly, it is worth noting that the moving average, when used, must be adopted together with other technical analysis tools such as candlestick analysis or graphical configurations, in fact they alone are not sufficient to set up a valid trading strategy because they have some defects, for instance they provide delayed signals to enter the market and can generate false operational signals that can cause significant losses.

Image 1.27: Crossing of two moving averages, one with 50 periods and the other with 20 periods

RSI

The relative force index is one of the most widely used oscillators in all technical analysis. The formula with which it is calculated is the following: RSI=100-(100/(1+Rs)), where Rs is the average of closings of the last n days. As for the latter, their number can be adjusted freely by the analyst, but many studies have confirmed that the timeframe that best suits this type of indicator is 14 days. The value of the relative strength index ranges between 0 and 100, within which there is an area of overbought (70-100) and one of oversold (0-30). RSI is capable of supplying various operating signals: the main one is that it allows the investor to anticipate the bounces and the corrections when it enters in the zones of overbought and oversold; moreover it allows to detect potential changes of feeling from the trader through the formation of positive or negative divergences; finally in trend phases, when the oscillator is found in the phases of overbought or oversold, it provides analysts with a confirmation of the current trend.

In the image below it appears evident that when RSI enters the overbought/oversold zones, from then on, there is a trend reversal with even important corrections that, if followed, can bring profits. From an operating point of view it is however always better to wait for some signal that confirms what is indicated by the oscillator, such as the formation of a candle or a reversal pattern.

Image 1.28: 14-periods RSI

Macd

The Macd, which stands for Moving Average Convergence-Divergence, is an important indicator used in technical analysis. It is made up of two moving averages with different speeds and a fixed centre line called the 0 line. Unlike the relative strength index, it has no overbought or oversold areas; therefore it will not provide signals of that type. The two averages that make up the mad they are: the signal line, which is the fastest average and is generated as the difference between an exponential moving average at 26 days and one at 12 days; and the trigger line, which is the slowest exponential average set at 9 days, calculated on the values of the signal line. The mad, like all other indicators and oscillators, allows the analyst to adjust it as he pleases, a trader can choose to change the duration of the trigger line from 9 days to 5 days if he thinks it is more appropriate. The above mentioned periods are the most applied to this indicator. From an operational point of view the mad provides the following operational cues:

- A bullish signal, when the fastest average, i.e. the signal line cuts from the bottom up the trigger line.
- A bearish signal, when the signal line cuts from top to bottom the trigger line.
- A bullish signal when the signal line from bottom to top cuts the 0 line.
- A bearish signal when the signal line cuts the 0 line from top to bottom.
- It enables to find possible divergences in the evolution of prices, thus allowing operators to anticipate market movements.

An important point to make is that the mad alone is not sufficient to create a winning trading strategy, so the signals it provides must be combined with confirmation from Japanese candles or graphical configurations. Finally, it must be emphasized that when the signal provided by the interaction of the signal line with the trigger line occurs at the intersection of the 0 line, the signal is particularly strong; it can thus be followed even without any confirmation from other indicators.

The histogram shown in the figure below is used to represent the distance between the signal line and the trigger line, which is why when the two moving averages intersect it is always equal to 0. Its purpose is to signal when the trend is weakening; indeed as the uptrend reduces the histogram approaches the 0 line, similarly it happens when the downtrend decreases.

Image 1.29: Macd 12, 26, 9

Bollinger Bands

Another set of indicators that is worth mentioning for its great success within the financial markets is the Bollinger Bands, invented by the famous analyst John Bollinger. From a graphic point of view, the Bollinger bands are composed of three lines: a central moving average with 20 periods used to indicate the short term trend in which the market is located; and then two bands, one upper and one lower which widen or narrow according to the volatility observed on the market. These bands are built by adding and subtracting from the moving average the value of the standard deviation, then multiplied by two, the latter measures the dispersion of the values with respect to the reference average. Like all the other indicators, in the Bollinger Bands the reference period can be set by the analyst according to his way of operating.

From an operating perspective, the indicator is used to:

- Identify any volatility compressions, which are reported by the indicator when bands tighten around prices. When you find that kind of situation it means the market is close to a directional phase.
- Confirm a possible ongoing trend, this happens when prices remain in contact with the upper band in the case of a bullish movement, or lower in the case of a bearish phase.
- Foresee a correction or a potential inversion of the trend, when prices come out of one of the two bands, thus highlighting a phase

in which either excess demand or excess supply has occurred.

Image 1.30: 20-period Bollinger Bands

For those who wish to deepen technical analysis, surely the most detailed and complete book to learn technical analysis from scratch is "*Technical Analysis of Financial Markets*" by J.J. Murphy.

Chapter 2

Psychology in technical analysis

2.1 Prospect theory

Various statistical studies have found that only 10% of traders make a profit, while the remaining 90% either fail to earn or lose money. So why is it that only 1 in 10 can make a profit on the stock market? The answer to this question does not lie in the knowledge of technical analysis, but in the psychology behind financial investments.

In this regard, it is interesting to mention the prospect theory, developed by two Israeli psychologists, Amos Tversky and Daniel Kahneman, at the end of the 1970s. According to this theory the choices of human beings in financial matters systematically violate the principles of rationality; this is mainly due to two related phenomena:

- The framing effect: These are the effects of the context within which subjects make their individual choices. This depends on numerous factors such as the education received, individual ideals, the appetite for risk and the mental situation of the person in question. Thus, this phenomenon explains why some individuals who are in the same situation of choice see possible diametrically opposed solutions. In the case of technical analysis it is explained with the framing effect the existence of the market, that is the place where supply and demand meet, and various individuals who have the same objective take opposite choices at the same time.

- Loss aversion: This phenomenon explains why for many people the motivation to avoid a certain loss is greater than the motivation to make a possible gain. This means that in our mind the loss of a sum of money has a greater influence than earning the same amount. Let's suppose that we currently have two open positions, one with a profit of 25 euros and the other with a loss of 50 euros, most people who do not know the psychological rules behind the financial investments will think about closing the 25 euros position immediately, for fear of losing the gains achieved, while they will leave the one with a loss of 50 euros open, because they will have the hope of recovering the money they are losing. If you look at the situation from a rational and objective point of view you can understand that in reality it was better for the trader to close the loss-making one immediately, because it meant that the market was moving in the opposite direction and leave open the profit position that was following the trend. The aversion to the loss explains therefore the reason for which the individuals prefer to hold back the losses and to take the profits immediately.

If a trader wants to become successful, he must therefore know thoroughly the psychological state in which he will find himself in the course of his operations, and only through a conscious management of his emotions will he be able to develop the winning attitude, i.e. the attitude to victory in which only that 10% of traders who are successful in the financial markets have.

2.2 Emotions in trading

Operating within the financial markets generates strong emotions in investors who see, second after second, changes in the capital they have set for their investments, and the more this capital is substantial, the more investments will be important and the stronger the emotions will be. The secret of a successful trader is not hidden in his knowledge of technical analysis, which however plays a fundamental role in the interpretation of financial markets, but in his ability to absolute master his emotions, regardless of what happens to his capital.

Positive emotions in trading

The positive emotions generated by the study of financial markets are a tool that the trader must use with rationality in order to become a successful trader, which are:

- Joy: Certainly joy is the emotion that *par excellence* must be present in the mind of every successful trader, it does not derive as a consequence of the positive results that the trader finds within the market, but arises even earlier, precisely when the trader starts the analysis of the chart. Basically, this emotion must take space in the mind of the individual from the moment he performs an activity that he loves and is passionate about, as a result it will be easier to achieve desired results, but also overcome moments of difficulty. If the investor then likes to analyse the markets, and these lead him to a profit, then this will create a positive momentum that will lead the individual to become a successful trader. A final observation to be made about joy is that the trader will have to be careful that this does not turn into euphoria, thus making him mistakenly believe that he is a seer and can therefore always predict the performance of the markets. This arrogance will inexorably lead to open numerous positions, even if the market does not provide clear operational cues; perhaps even without the placement of an appropriate stop loss, thus leading the analyst to major losses and a possible ruin of the available capital.

- Calmness: One of the key traits of a successful trader is calmness, this allows him to have a more rational and objective view of what is happening in the markets and to his capital. Most of the work activities are based on the idea that the more time dedicated to work will lead to more potential gain. In the world of technical analysis this mentality becomes deleterious and can lead to huge losses, in fact in trading it is not said that the more positions you open the more you will gain; indeed, it would be enough to open even a single position per month to have a substantial gain. The successful investor will therefore have to be calm to be able to identify the most interesting ideas that arise within the market, and avoid opening positions that arise from the frantic activity on the stock exchange, it is said that the work of the analyst is a job of quality and not quantity. Finally, calmness will also be essential to keep cool and rational when you have positions in profit, in order to be able to counteract that desire to cash in immediately after a few gains, without allowing them to develop further.

Negative emotions in trading

Negative emotions that arise when operating in financial markets, lead operators to strong tensions that lead them to wrong analysis because carried out with poor clarity and coldness, such emotions are:

- Greed: This emotion rises when the trader closes a profitable position, but later he realizes that if he kept it open he could earn more money. This emotion is disastrous for analysts, because if you experience a feeling of unhappiness even when you have made a profit it will be difficult for the trader to feel positive emotions, because entering at the beginning of a trend and leaving at the end is virtually impossible. Such negative feelings over time will affect the ability to analyse the markets with lucidity and objectivity, thus leading the trader to a series of negative trades that will transport him into a vicious circle, which could cost him the entire capital. Greed also manifests itself when the trader decides not to close a profitable trade because he hopes to earn more even if the charts show signs of reversal. In this case the greed will induce the operator to lose the gains achieved, and in the worst case scenario, to close the operation in loss. From a psychological point of view this event will have devastating effects on the investor's morale, causing him a great disappointment. In order to prevent greed from taking a hold on the trader's mind, he needs to learn to interpret the charts and not to hope that they will move in the desired direction.
- Stagnation: The trader experiences this emotion whenever prices are not heading in the desired direction. When you find yourself in this

situation you feel insecure and unable to make a decision, as a result you will let prices run without intervening in any way hoping that in the future they will move in the hoped-for direction. This type of behaviour is catastrophic both for the analyst's operations and for his capital, because sometimes the financial instrument moves in favour of the operator, while other times it can lead to lose profits or suffer serious losses. In order to avoid being a victim of immobility, the trader, before opening every single position, needs to plan every detail precisely and accurately so that he is ready for any situation ahead of him.

- Fear: This emotion is always present in the trader; one is afraid of having opened a wrong position, of having placed the stop loss badly, of losing the gains obtained and of not achieving the desired results. Fear therefore accompanies the trader in every moment of his operations, but the successful analyst is aware that this emotion is always with him, he must learn to control and manage it, because being afraid of the market is right, otherwise the trader would feel like a seer thinking he can interpret each chart and always be right. However, it must be pointed out that the investor should not be overwhelmed by fear, otherwise he could commit acts that have no justification, or he could avoid opening potential positions that would lead him to gain. Let's make an example: an analyst opens a long position, but the prices start to fall towards the previously placed stop loss, then the trader for fear of losing more money closes the position just before the stop, but since it was placed correctly the prices undergo a trend reversal and go back in the direction that the trader had identified, although he will not enjoy it in any way. In order to control the fear, and use it to his own advantage, the trader will have to strictly follow the strategies and plans he established without being influenced by all those feelings that arise from the fear of losing money.

- Desperation: This emotion occurs when the investor suffers a consecutive series of losses, which not only damage his capital, but also ruin his mind by making him lose self-confidence. Such feelings will lead him to open other positions, but without being convinced of how he is operating, he will leave them to chance and luck, which rarely reward in the world of technical analysis. To avoid desperation the trader will have to face losses, even if they're consecutive, as a physiological element of his operations, being aware that they will always be present within his analysis, in fact many successful analysts recommend seeing losses as the cost of any business activity.

2.3 EGO

With the term ego we generally mean our own person and the awareness of who we are. Some successful traders, say that to be successful in the field of technical analysis and not be influenced by the many emotions that invade the trader, he must be able to destroy his own ego, so as to be able to observe with complete lucidity the movements of prices. Specifically, this trading philosophy says that the ego leads the analyst to compete with the market and challenge it, so any possible loss will be seen by the trader as an insult to his intelligence and will hurt his pride. The fact is that the market of how we are and what we think does not give a damn at all. Such feelings will consequently lead the investor to want to quickly recover the losses, even if the market does not offer the right opportunities, this will lead to new mistakes, pushing him into a very dangerous loop for his available capital. The successful trader on the other hand knows that he does not have to prove anything either to himself or to the highs, so he will be able to accept a loss without feeling the irrepressible need to recover it as soon as possible. This theory also argues that the successful analyst should not believe what he thinks, but only what he sees, in fact he should not be influenced by his own thoughts, which are part of the ego and therefore of who we are, because they may have been conditioned by many external factors and therefore lead to a non-transparent view of the market. The only thing the trader has to rely on is the price chart, because only the price chart allows you to really understand what is happening in the market and gives you the possibility to estimate what will happen in the future.

Chapter 3

10 laws to control the market

This chapter is undoubtedly the key part of the book, and you will hardly find it in other books, as the following 10 rules are the result of years of experience and study that have enabled me to control the market. It is precisely in CONTROL that the success of great traders lies, because only this allows us to always be masters of what we do. The CONTROL is divided into *market control* and *self-control*.

The former enables us to analyse the graphs and manage the positions we have in our portfolio through the appropriate use of all the tools offered by technical analysis, fundamental analysis and money management.
The latter enables us to deal with our emotionality and to operate calmly without the anxiety that very often leads us to make hasty and irrational choices, which in trading become easily lethal.
The following 10 rules have not been listed in order of importance, as they are all essential for full control of your investments. Indeed, it is necessary that they are integrated with each other, thus creating a synergy of skills and attention that will not only help you improving your performance in the markets, but above all to be able to live trading with the mental lucidity that defines the boundary between those who lose money and those who make profit.

1: *Always follow the main trend*

The first of the ten laws that I want to present is undoubtedly essential to increase your chances of success in online trading. More than a law for those who make trading, it can almost be defined as the very essence of trading, namely **ALWAYS FOLLOW THE MAIN TREND.**

As we have seen in chapter 1.4 the trend can have three directions, what the trader must do is to determine the underlying trend, i.e. the primary price direction, and then open only positions favouring this trend. So, for example, if the primary trend is bullish I will open only upward positions, if it is bearish only downward. With this I do not want to say that it is not possible to make counter-trend operations, but should they be made the advice is always to reduce the exposure in such operations, because the probabilities to take a loss are considerably higher.

What if it is a sideways trend?

In this case you can do two things:

- Hold on to that particular tool and wait for signals to confirm the movement of a trend.

- Exploit the price sideways to open long or short positions.

Let's look into this last point:

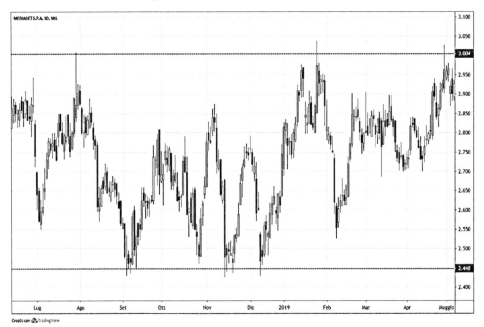

Image 3.1: Media set stock sideways trend

The above is the Media set S.P.A chart on a 24 hour time frame, it is the same image presented in chapter 1.4. As you can see the prices in the last year have moved laterally between the level of 3.004 and 2.448. The strategy a trader can use in this case is as follows:

- Open downward positions when prices reach 3,004, with stop at closing above 3,004, protective stop at 3,100 and target 2,448.

- Open upward positions when prices reach 2,448, with stop at closing above 2,448, protective stop at 2,400 and target 3,004.

The argument on the closing stop and protective stop is discussed in chapter 3.7. The above strategy has a very good risk/return ratio and if the market's sideways nature lasts for a medium to long period of time it can bring excellent results.

Going back to the point of following of the main trend, often people ask me if there is a method in order to identify it without errors and without risking to be influenced from retracements or false signals.

The answer: SURE. It can be done by using the tools that are provided to us from the technical analysis that I have described in chapter one. Before explaining the method I would like to emphasize that the type of trading must always be related to the reference time frame. That is if I trade at 1 hour the chart that I will take into consideration to determine the underlying trend will be the 1 hour chart not the 4 hour chart or daily, on the contrary if I swing trading, so I keep the positions open for a few days, I will consider the daily candlestick chart. By this I do not mean that you should not look at the weekly charts if you are swing trading, but you should focus on the daily chart, because the weekly chart is nothing more than the aggregation of the daily chart, so I think the most sensible thing is to analyse the daily chart using the zoom.

Here is a practical example of how to determine a market trend:

Image 3.2: Daily chart of Netflix stock

Here is the Netflix stock chart and we are trying to determine the various trends that the stock has shown from the beginning of 2018 until January 2019.

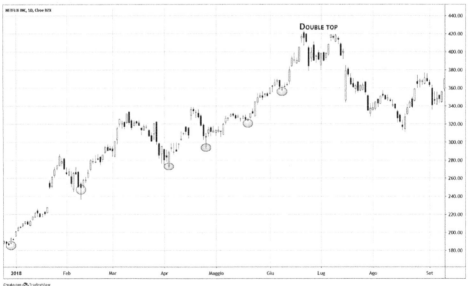
Image 3.3: Analysis of the uptrend and the double top of the Netflix share price

By zooming in we can see that from the beginning of 2018 until July 2018 prices have always marked increasing highs and lows, which I highlighted with ellipses. This means that until July I knew I was in a bullish trend, so I could have entered long, as after drawing the third ellipse I would have noticed that I was in a bullish market. Between mid-June and the beginning of July, however, I realized that something happened, prices stopped rising and drew a double high. The latter is a sign of a bearish inversion and makes me understand that the trend is changing from bullish to: I don't know, as it could become either lateral or bearish, let's look at the chart.

Image 3.4: Sideways trend and bearish trend analysis of Netflix stock

After having shaped and completed, through the break of the level of 380$, the double top, the prices from the beginning of July begin to move in a lateral trend, this is clear to me since the highs and lows are not updated. I highlight this sideways trend with a rectangle that starts in early July and ends in mid-October. The red flag that the sideways trend is finished is suggested to me by the downward breaking of the support that was the lower base of the rectangle. In the following days in fact the prices start to go down creating decreasing highs and lows, marked with small rectangles, until the end of 2018.

Just towards the end of the year the prices create an important pattern of inversion that is a bullish engulfing, in fact in the following days the price of the shares starts rising significantly.

Image 3.5: Complete Netflix stock analysis

The above figure is similar to the first image that I have inserted talking about Netflix, with the only difference that in this case I have described all the phases of the trend through ellipses, rectangles and short comments. Such system allows to have a clearer vision of the phase of market in which it is found, in fact if one looks at the previous diagram, it results of difficult interpretation; on the contrary, the above image is easy to interpret and allows us to understand immediately what stage of the trend we are in.

For this reason I recommend to all traders who wish to have full control of their trades to use the methodology just explained in order to have the clarity of mind that is necessary to understand in which direction prices are moving, and thus be able to trade always in favour of the main trend, thus increasing their chances of success.

2: *Earn more than you lose*

The second law is: earn more than you lose. You might say: *Bravo, don't tell me, you're a smart guy.* In reality the secret of technical analysis is just that.

In trading the wrong losses and investments are the norm, for this reason it is important that the analyst creates a proportion between the value of losses and profits.

Take two analysts as an example, trader A who out of 100 positions closes 70 in profit, and trader B who out of 100 trades closes only 30 in profit. At first glance it could be suggested that A is much more profitable than B, but this is not always true, because if A closes 70 positions in which he profits 2 euros and 30 in which he loses 5 euros at the end of the month, this analyst will have suffered losses even though 70% of the positions he opened were profitable. Conversely, trader B may have made a profit even if only 30 positions were profitable. Through this example it is easy to understand how key it is to create a proportion between profits and losses. The ratio recommended by many professionals is the 3:1, so that with only one trade in profit you can recover the losses of 3 others, but each analyst can choose to set his own proportion between stop loss and take profit based on his skills and his way of trading. Personally I prefer to use a proportion between 4:1 and 2:1, and when my operatively grants it to me I always choose to cut the losses when they are still small and they damage only mildly my capital. But that's just me.

Better to lose 10 euros today than 50 tomorrow.

With the example above I don't want to tell you that if the ratio you use is 1:1 you will surely lose money, but you will surely need a more sound analysis, which is not easy at all.

Warren Buffet, the best investor in the history of mankind, said: *"The first rule for those who operate on the stock exchange is: do not lose money, the second: never forget the first"*. Apart from the catchphrase there is a very precise reason why the number one rule of trading is not to lose money and it is hidden behind the **LAW OF STATISTICAL RUIN**.

The law of statistical ruin shows that the possibility of recovering the initial value of the lost capital is inversely proportional to the loss incurred. Let me clarify with an example:

I start trading with a capital of 1000 euros, I open a long position that unfortunately goes wrong and I do not put the stop loss because I start thinking *"it can't go down indefinitely"*, *"it will never happen"* etc. ... I leave my position open until I lose half of my capital, then with a glimmer of lucidity I close the long and I find myself with only € 500 on the account. Summing up, I have lost 50% of my capital, thus I have halved it with only one position. But now I want to recover it and with a stroke of luck I open a long position that goes well and increase my capital by 50%.
NOTE:

How much is 50% of 500?   500 x 50/100 = **250**

It means that now our total capital is $500 + 250 = 750$. So first losing 50% of my capital and then increasing my capital by 50% I find myself with 25% less than what I started, in fact in order to recover the entire loss suffered initially and return to 1000 euros I would have to earn 100% of my capital in fact: $500 + (500 \times 100/100) = 1000$.

From an economic point of view, therefore, the statistical ruin is very heavy for the trader, but do we want to analyse it from a psychological point of view? The trader who sees his account halved feels an insane amount of negative emotions, which start from anger for not having closed the position before, to sadness and loss of self-confidence for losing much of his money, until the worst moment: the discouragement and the desire to quit, which arises from the thought of how long it will take to recover all the money that has been lost.

The advice I feel like giving to those who are in this situation, since I myself have been in this situation several times, is the following: take a few days off from trading, do something else, and as soon as you feel ready come back in front of the monitor, but not with the desire to recover all the lost capital right away, but with the desire to get back in the game and learn. So don't consider the time you are spending on trading after a serious loss as lost time, but as time you are spending on your training, understand where and why you made a mistake and make sure it won't happen again. You are just gaining experience. As Oscar Wilde said: "experience is just the name we give to our mistakes".

The law of statistical ruin is therefore devastating for traders, both economically and psychologically, and that is why it becomes so difficult to be profitable on the stock exchange, the only way to stem this problem is to always control losses with proper stop management, which I will discuss in the seventh law.

Do not worry, however, there are also virtuous loops in the world of trading and the most famous and relevant of these is certainly the compound interest which allows you to multiply your earnings over the years. This system is often used in banks' investment funds, but it can also be applied to the trading world, with the only difference that in this case you decide how to invest your money.

How does compound interest work?

It works that in addition to accruing interest in the first year of investment, in subsequent years it will be calculated not only on the initial capital, but on the capital + interest, so you will earn interest on interest. Let's make a practical example:

I start trading with 10,000€ and the first year I earn 20% of my initial capital, so at the end of the year I will have 12,000€. Now I have two options to choose from: either I withdraw the 2000€ earned and continue trading with the initial 10,000, or I continue the following year trading with 12,000€ without withdrawing.

Let's say that the following year I earn another 20% from my trading investments: if I have 10,000€ I go back to 12,000€, but if I start with

12,000€ and earn 20% at the end of the year I have 14,400€, so 400€ more than if I had withdrawn the 2000€ earned the previous year.

Let's extend this example to 10 years, assuming we earn a 20% profit each year:

- If you withdraw the profits you earn 2000€ for 10 years at the end you have cashed 20.000€.

- If you do not withdraw the profits your earnings will be as follows: .000+2.400+2.880+3.456+4.147+4.977+5.972+7.166+8.600+10.320= 51.918€.

The difference after 10 years is therefore 51.918 - 20.000 = 31.918€. This is a remarkable and very relevant difference for each current account, for this reason I always advise traders not to withdraw the earned profits immediately, but to keep them on the account in order to use the compound interest. Warren Buffet himself is considered the best investor in the world not because he doubles his capital every month, but because he uses compound interest, the only difference is that he does it with billions of dollars.

A last piece of advice that can be extrapolated from this example is definitely about time, in fact, the more time you have the more you can exploit the compound interest, so it is very important to START INVESTING WHEN YOU'RE YOUNG, because you have a lot, tons of time on your side.

3: *Supports and resistances are price ranges*

The third law is of vital importance to make precise technical analysis and is the following: SUPPORTS AND RESISTANCES ARE PRICE RANGES. In many manuals these are represented as lines and therefore a novice reader thinks that supports and resistances are only price levels for example 55$ for the oil, instead very often they're actually price ranges, in the case of the oil could therefore be between 54,5$ and 55,5$.

Therefore the advice I would give to traders who are used to drawing horizontal lines with poor results is to represent the supports and resistances with rectangles as in the following examples.

EUR/GBP CASE

Image 3.6: Support on EUR/GBP chart

This is the euro/pound forex exchange rate, 24 hours time frame. From the chart above we can see that my support is represented by a horizontal straight line at the level of 0.84909 and we can also see that prices have broken this support several times during the session, but have always closed above this level.

Looking at this image the first thing that comes to mind to a trader who trusts the books he has studied is that the market, due to the high volatility, has created many false breaks. IT'S NOT LIKE THAT!!

What have the prices really done?

Prices have always bounced on the support simply in some cases they have taken the top of the support, in others the bottom.

Then why did I identify the support in area 0.84909?

The answer is that I put it a little bit randomly... Let me explain.

The support is not the horizontal line 0.84909, but it is the whole area from 0.84952 to 0.84738.

Image 3.7: Supportive area on the EUR/GBP chart

Why then in many books is it represented with a tuition?

It is represented with a straight line because experienced traders generally prefer a clean chart and choose to draw a straight line instead of drawing a rectangle, but they know very well that **SUPPORTS AND RESISTANCES ARE PRICE BUNDS**.

Throughout this book I will also show charts where the supports and resistances will be represented by straight lines, but keep in mind that they are always areas.

PETROLEUM CASE

Now that we have defined supports and resistances as areas of our chart that can be identified with rectangles, it remains for us to understand how to make the most of them in our operations.

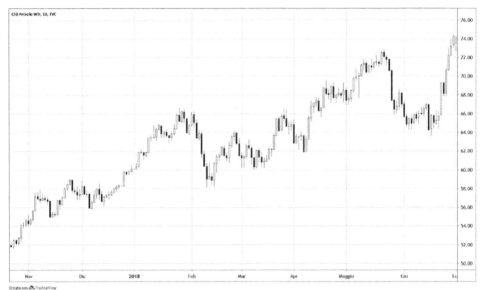
Image 3.8: Daily oil chart

The image above is the daily chart of oil, analyzing it we notice that we are in a clear bullish trend characterized by increasing highs and lows. Let's imagine that we are in front of this chart and we want to go upward on oil, but surely the level of 74$ touched by prices at the end of June is too high, so we must identify a support to be able to position ourselves upward. So we are waiting for a price retracement in order to get a better risk/return ratio.

How do we identify the support where we would like to enter?

First, as shown in the previous case, we must look for an area where prices have bounced several times in the past.

Image 3.9: I identified the areas where prices have bounced back

By zooming in the chart I notice that between $64 and $65 there is an area where prices have bounced several times, precisely three, in fact once this area has worked as a support, then worked twice as resistance.

Someone with an attentive eye now might ask me why I do not choose the area around $66.50, indeed even in that area prices have bounced several times. The reason why I prefer support in the $64 area is because it has never been broken by prices, while the $66 area has already been broken several times precisely two times, i.e. before the rebounds in the $64 area.

Image 3.10: Evidence of the supportive area

Now we only have to highlight the area by means of a rectangle. This rectangle, in order to be drawn correctly, will have to include most of the shadows of the candles that have hit the price area we are interested in.

In our specific case the supportive area we are interested in ranges from $63.98 to $64.88.

What should we do at this point?

We just have to **wait** for prices to return to the area highlighted by us, in order to position ourselves upwards in favour of the main trend.

Image 3.11: The prices come back to test my support

After a little more than a month oil prices came back down again and hit the supportive area we were monitoring on drawing a small bullish candle, so I decided to enter with a protective stop loss in the $63.98 area and stop loss at closing prices below the $63.98 level. (Protective stop loss and stop loss at closing prices will be discussed in the seventh law). My targets are: first the $67.50 level, then the $70 level, and finally the previous highs in the $75 area. These are all levels where there are old supports that have turned into resistances because they were broken by prices.

PLEASE NOTE: Right when I decided to enter, prices hit my supportive area and just at that moment (in those two days) they showed indecision closing always above the level of $64.88, so they confirmed the effectiveness of the supportive area highlighted by me.

Image 3.12: Oil chart after my long entry

In the following days the prices start rising again and in less than 15 days they reach both the first and the second target, so I take home part of my position and let the last third one run to the final target, which is reached after one month. I will expand this last part on the fractionation of the position in point 6, for the moment it is enough to have understood how to identify and how to make the best use of the areas where there are supports and static resistances.

4: *Work easy, few indicators*

The fourth law is especially important for less experienced but very willing traders. I say this because many trading books explain many indicators: moving averages, Bollinger bands, RSI, MACD and many others. *What effect does this have on traders?*

It has the consequence that traders, trusting the manual, start to have charts with at least 3 different indicators and every time they see a position open, and unfortunately 90% of the time they lose money. There are several reasons for this, for example, with regard to moving averages the signal is often delayed, or if the RSI is in the oversold or overbought zone it does not force prices to go up or down, but they can safely continue their trend. I do not want to linger too much on this because this is not the end of the chapter, but it is to avoid the trader falling into this situation...

Image 3.13: Gold daily chart with three set indicators

The above graph is the gold on time frame daily. Inside the chart I inserted 3 indicators: RSI at 14 periods, MACD (12,26,9), and Bollinger bands 20,2.

In a chart like the one above it is difficult to make analysis, because the different indicators present provide too much information that leads the analyst to make mistakes, or at least create huge confusion that takes away lucidity and therefore money. Moreover, the different indicators at certain times give discordant signals, let's see an example.

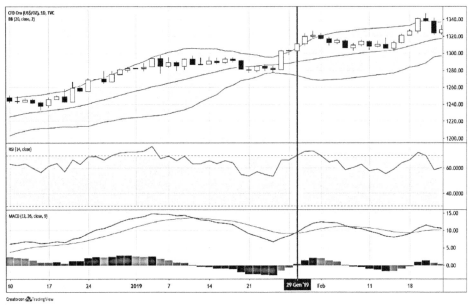

Image 3.14: Contrasting signals on the daily gold chart

The chart above is always the gold on a daily time frame, I simply zoomed in the image to show you a classic example where various indicators give discordant signals. On January 29th our chart gives us the following information:

-RSI in overbought area, *bearish signal.*

-MACD with the fastest straight line intersecting the slowest upward, bullish *signal.*

-Bollinger bands where the upper band has been broken by rising prices, *bearish signal.*

Summing up, we have set 3 different indicators that give us conflicting signals... well; very well... it's official: we don't know what to do!

What should a trader do in such a situation?

The best thing you can do is to delete all these indicators. Trading is already difficult enough by its nature and there is no need to complicate it even further. It is the same thing as they do in soccer schools to children, if you are not good with your feet play easy, low ball and you will certainly make fewer mistakes. In trading it is the exact same thing: WORK EASY.

What should I study about the graph then?

The PRICE, the PRICE and again the PRICE, because it is precisely the PRICE that tells us how the markets are moving, the indicators are nothing but representations of prices. It is like when you have to meet a boy or a girl; do you prefer to meet them in person or write them on Facebook looking at their profile all tweaked?

The indicators are like photoshop, they deceive you, make you doubt and hardly show you what reality is really like.

Therefore, the best thing to do is to delete all these indicators/oscillators, keep a clean chart and observe price movements carefully.

We review the case of gold between mid-August 2018 and early March 2019 without using any indicator.

Image 3.15: Price analysis on the gold chart

Compared to the previous chart full of indicators, the latter is much cleaner and also easier to read and interpret.

The first thing you notice is the presence of a morning star in the middle of August, the latter is a bullish signal that must make you think of a potential change in trend. Such inversion is confirmed in the following days, in fact the prices after a phase of laterality that begins at the end of August until the end of September start to rise strongly and in the following months they mark increasing highs and lows. The trend continues until the middle of March until an evening star is formed on the chart, a particularly important bearish signal that brings prices down in the following days. I would like to underline that both the reversal signals are presented with important volumes, not a case because in the world of trading in most cases, not in all, the signal that a trend is finished and another is about to start is confirmed by the presence of important volumes.

Now let's re-examine the previous case, where we had set the three indicators that gave us conflicting signals and consequently led us to great confusion.

Image 3.16: Price study where indicators showed conflicting signals

In studying the prices the first thing we notice is that these stay within a sideways trend from the beginning of the year until the end of January, highlighted by the rectangle in figure.

What do you do when you are inside a rectangle?

Either you exploit it by buying at the bottom of the rectangle and selling at the top, or you wait for it to do a breakout on top or down to position yourself in the direction the prices are heading. In our case the prices are within a main medium term bullish trend, they break the rectangle upwards, so the most sensible thing to do is to enter long with stop at the closing of prices below the bottom of the rectangle. This shows how studying prices is always better than using indicators and oscillators that risk confusing the trader to a distorted view of the market.

5: *Do not anticipate the market*

Many novice traders, fresh out of manuals and hours of study often try to anticipate the market, to anticipate it. Unfortunately, the market does not give a damn at all of what we think and what we believe, on the contrary, it can often give us false signals that may lead us to open positions and lose a lot of money. As U.S. economist John Kenneth Galbraith said *"The function of economic forecasts is to make astrology seem respectable"*. Never phrase was truer.

The question that surely arises at this point is:

"If I can't predict the markets then why am I studying trading?"

Here the difference is subtle, but fundamental. The trader does not want to predict the market. I do not care if oil in ten years will cost $ 500 per barrel or $ 5 per barrel, I cannot know and I will not be able to predict it even with all the data in the world. What I am interested in identifying is the trend when I analyse the charts, identify the best entry level and ride the trend as much as possible.

Identifying the best level of entry is the part where many traders make mistakes and it costs them dearly. The reason they make mistakes is that they want to anticipate the market, foresee it. THE MARKET SHOULD NEVER BE ANTICIPATED.

I've heard many traders say: *"surely from that level you will see that it will tip over and you will go back up again"*. In this sentence there are two mistakes: the first one is that for sure there is never anything in trading, that is why you should always be cautious and account for losses, the second one is that the level our friend was talking about has been broken by prices and he burnt half the account.

A rule that I always apply when I want to enter on a particular financial instrument is to ***always wait for the daily closing***, because I operate and analyse the daily charts, for those who use lower time frame charts the point does not change. I have decided to integrate this rule to my operations because very often during a day there can be false signals from the prices, for example false breakages of supports or resistances, to avoid being a victim of these issues, I prefer to analyse and decide whether or not to enter the market only at the end of the day and candlelight drawn.

So how do I know when to enter the market?

When you want to enter into position on a particular financial instrument the best thing to do is to identify the most important price levels.

In the past I made many mistakes trying unnecessarily to anticipate prices, but my operation improved only when I understood the importance of identifying certain price levels, such as supports and resistances, and waiting for the **end of the daily closure** prices to give me some signal that the support or resistance had worked.

I'll explain myself better with an example:

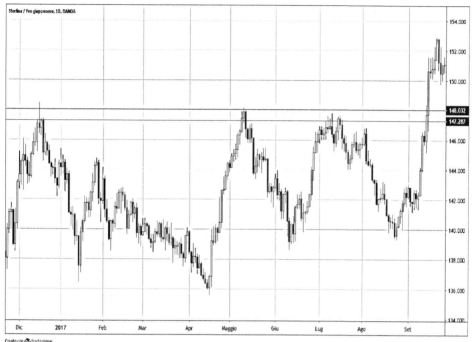

Image 3.17: Resistance area on daily chart GBP/JPY

We are on the daily GBP/JPY chart, prices have bounced several times on the resistance area between 148.03 and 147.28 (I am talking about the resistance area as explained in the third law). In mid-September this area is strongly broken by prices which draw new highs. To this point I am eager to enter the rise, but I want to wait for the better moment, that is a return in the highlighted area which has gone from being a zone of resistances to being a supportive level.

Image 3.18: Prices return to my supportive area

In the following days the prices start to go down and they go right back to my supportive area, in fact they almost break it. **This is not the time to enter long**, because it is true that prices are back to test the level, but they did not "tell" me that the support is working, indeed they seem determined to go down again.

Image 3.19: Prices bounce on my supportive area

The following day the prices draw a bullish candle that seems to show a good strength from the buyers, also this candle is drawn right where I had traced my support. THIS IS THE MOMENT TO ENTER LONG, as the condition I prefer occurs:

Support or Resistance + Candle favourable to my analysis

Image 3.20: Daily chart analysis GBP/JPY

In the following days we enjoy a good rise until the beginning of November where we create a shooting star that brings the prices close to the supportive area.

It is interesting to note that at the end of November we create a new bullish candle right next to our supportive area and the situation we prefer to enter the market, support + confirmation candle and consequently we go back up again, getting profit from our operation.

A last piece of advice I would like to give is that as soon as you realize that you have opened a position without the right analysis, but only by looking at the graph for a second your brain says: *"What an opportunity! "Open, open!!"*. The best thing to do is to get out of the market immediately whether you are in profit or loss, because the operations that arise from a rush of adrenaline hardly bring money into the account.

6: *Split the position*

What does splitting a position mean?

To **split a position** means liquidating a part of the negotiated contracts, then to close a part of the position that can be a 25%, a 33%, a 50% etc... This way the trader can guarantee himself a certain profit, of course if prices continue to move in the direction in which he is positioned he will give up a part of the profit.

Splitting the position is definitely a great way to keep control of your operations in the market. It enables us to constantly control our exposure, as it is precisely the latter that brings anxiety and stress to traders. For example, if I buy a barrel of oil whose price goes from $100 to $50 in a day I do not worry, as I lost only $50, but if instead of buying one I buy 1000 barrels, even with the slightest movement of the oil price from $100 to $99 I get nervous, as it is $1000 that come out of my account in a few hours.

Let's suppose that we buy a thousand barrels, for some reason probably irrational due to an excess of euphoria, but after a few minutes that we are in position we get scared stiff and we cannot remain lucid in front of the screen. What do we do?

Over the years I've seen a lot of traders do this: remove all kinds of stops, turn off the pc and pray hard... How did it end? Sometimes well, maybe they even made a profit, other times...they halved their balance. Of course this is not the right thing to do; if you think you are too exposed the best thing to do is to immediately close a part of your position, then split it. Going back to the case of a thousand barrels, simply close 90% of your position and stay only with 100 barrels, this way you will be less exposed on the market and above all you will be more lucid and calm in front of the monitor, in other words: you will have regained control.

Splitting becomes very useful even when the market does not behave as you expect, i.e. when you lose confidence in your position. This is one of the most delicate situations for a trader, because if you do not believe in your trading yourself no one believes in it, as a result this insecurity often leads to trivial mistakes that cause inevitable losses of money.

Many traders when they study a financial instrument they monitor the chart until the moment they enter the position; then once they enter...shhhhhhh...the market for them immediately becomes mute. They no longer analyse the subsequent candles, but only hope that they move in the desired direction. In reality the chart is always changing and should be observed on a daily basis (if you study the daily charts, hour after hour if you trade on lower time frames), candlelight after candlelight because prices continue to move and then tell us how the market is moving. Let's analyse a real case:

Image 3.21: Bullish trend on the daily chart of the Nasdaq index

We are on the daily chart of the Nasdaq index. I realize that I am in a bullish trend marked by increasing highs and lows, I also identify a good supportive area in which to enter the market, which is hit by the prices, in particular the spinning top, the right end candle on the image, gives me confirmation that the support has worked, thus I enter long with protective stop loss at the level of 7231 and stop loss at the closing of prices below the bottom of the rectangle.

Image 3.22: I lighten the position on the Nasdaq index

After two days from my entry into the market prices form a particularly important indecision/reversal candle. It has a very long shadow, a sign that prices have risen throughout the day, but the body is very small, so all the bullish movement has been reabsorbed by the market. This situation causes me particular indecision and I lose confidence in my bullish position, so to be able to sleep peacefully and keep control of my operations without being affected by stress I decide to close 50% of my position, not all because my support has not yet been broken.

Image 3.23: Recovery of the bullish trend on the Nasdaq index

In the following days, the prices resume their ascent surpassing even the previous highs and I am able to bring home a good profit. Surely if I hadn't closed a part of the position I would have profited more, but I wouldn't have had the same peace of mind, so I prefer to reduce the profit, to be able to operate with the necessary calm to earn.

The most important function of splitting certainly concerns the targets, in fact it is important to split them and not have only one final target, but to have more targets on the graph. Personally when I enter the market I position at least two or three targets, so as to guarantee myself a profit, reduce exposure and at the same time let the prices run. The situation that I prefer when I position the targets is the following:

- First target: I close 35% of my position

-Second target: I close a second 35% of my position

-Third target: I close 25%/30% of my position, I write 25% because in case it is positioned on shares of companies where I see an important potential I always choose to leave a 5% for the long term.

Let's look at a real example:

Image 3.24: Choice of targets on the oil case

We are on the case of oil seen in the third rule, to summarize, without explaining the analysis because it has already been illustrated in point three, we entered long buying 100 barrels of oil at the closing of the candle highlighted by the ellipse, and we defined three targets: $ 67.49, $ 70.01 and $ 75.10. These three levels were chosen because they correspond to important supports and resistances that have worked in the past.

Respecting the scheme illustrated above, I split my position in this way:

-I closed 35 barrels as soon as prices reached the level of $67.49

-I closed another 35 barrels of the 65 I had left once prices hit the $70.01 level.

-I closed the last 30 barrels when the price of oil reached $75.10.

A further situation in which position splitting can be useful is certainly before any important news comes out. This can move the market strongly creating high volatility and a high probability of losing the profit from a well thought out transaction in a few seconds. So in these situations it is a good idea to close a part of the position and leave only 40/50% at the mercy of the news. Through this simple shrewdness if the news is in our favour we inflate our account well, on the contrary, if it is unfavourable we have already cashed in a part of the profit that we had achieved.

The last topic I want to deal with before moving on to the seventh rule is mediation, i.e. when a trader increases his exposure on a financial instrument that he has already bought and which is going down, in order to mediate the initial entry price. Let's make a practical example: our friend decides to buy a share at 30€ and instead of fixing a stop he decides to buy that share again every time it goes down by 2€, because he thinks: *imagine if it will be worth less than 10€.* So the inexperienced trader will buy at 28€ then at 26€, then at 24€ until the price goes down, *because it won't go as low as 10€,* but what if it *does*?

If it does get there, our friend has 11 positions at a loss with a large amount of capital invested without any certainty that prices will rise.

Surely it was better to take the stop, because in trading losses are inevitable, they are part of the game and must be seen as costs that you have to incur to run your business. Through this example it is clear that mediation is one of the fastest ways to destroy your trading account, which is why I strongly advise against it.

7: *Stop loss at candle closure and protective stop loss*

What are ***stop loss at a candle closure*** and ***protective stop loss***?

These two terms were invented by me. Of course I am not the only trader who uses this strategy, but for the sake of clarity in the explanation I decided to give a name to both of them. Over the years these two types of stops have helped me to always safeguard my capital without ever losing control of a trade.

We immediately give a definition of both terms in order to facilitate the explanation of both concepts.

Stop loss at closing prices: This stop loss is not a stop loss set on the trading platform, but it is a mental stop loss that the trader must have in case the closing prices of the day break a particular previously set level such as a support, resistance or trend line. The objective of this stop loss is to avoid suffering silly losses. Anyone who trades must have placed, at some point, the classic stop which was hit by prices at a time of high volatility, to then go back to what was originally thought, by the end of the day. In practice, instead of earning 50€ you lost 30€ just because volatility screwed you. The stop at the close of prices enables us to avoid this situation by closing the position manually at the close of the candle. There are two reasons why I always wait until the candle closes to close the position or not:

-avoid being a victim of false signals from the market.

- have a clearer view of what is happening on the graph.

Protective stop loss: This stop loss is the classic automatic stop that all platforms offer. In my approach I do not set this stop according to the technical analysis, but according to how much money I am prepared to lose on every operation that I do; in my case a 1% of all the capital that I have. Naturally if the level in which I set my protective stop loss matches with a good technical level, all the better, but otherwise the safeguard of the capital always prevails.

We see how to apply the stop loss to the closing of the prices and the protective stop loss to a real trading case.

Image 3.25: I identify the bearish trend on the GBP/USD exchange rate

We are on GBP/USD exchange rate on a 24 hour time frame. Through the study of the trend seen in the first law we see this is full bearish trend, we want to enter short on the exchange rate, selling British pound and buying American dollar.

Image 3.26: I identify the resistance area on the GBP/USD exchange rate

In the following days the British pound starts to appreciate against the dollar, so I am looking for a good level to position myself at a lower level in order to follow the main trend. The level that interests me is surely the area of resistance around the level of 1.2750 that I have highlighted with the rectangle in the picture.

Image 3.27: I set the protective stop loss and the stop loss at the closing of the prices

After a couple of days the prices go back inside the area I highlighted and at the end of the day they draw a doji, candle of uncertainty/inversion, so I decide to enter short.

Where do I place the stop loss?

I set the stop loss at the closing of the prices above the top of the rectangle, this means that at the end of the day I will go to see where the price has reached the exchange rate, and if this is higher than the corresponding price the top of the rectangle I will close the position, on the contrary I will leave it open.

On the other hand, I set the protective stop loss at the 1,28020 level which has no technical reason, but simply coincides with 1% of my capital, so if this level was hit I would lose 1% of my trading account.

Image 3.28: Prices hit my stop at closing prices, but close below it

The next day the prices go down strongly and therefore we are already in profit with our position, but we carefully analyse the candle of June 25 highlighted with the ellipse.

A trader which just ended his studies, following his manual correctly, would have placed the stop loss (I mean the automatic platform stop loss) above the maximum doji. However, he would have been impressed by the June 25th candle, as the day was highly volatile and prices went well above the doji high, and then closed the day well below it.

Image 3.29: The dollar continues to appreciate against sterling

In this case, as in many others, the stop loss at the closing of prices avoided a silly loss and allowed us to earn a lot of money. Indeed, as you can see from the image above, the price in the following month drops rapidly, and if a trader knows how to manage the position well by splitting the targets correctly as seen in the sixth law he could earn a lot of money by always having full control of the market.

A question that has often been asked to me when I explain this strategy is: *"Why use the protective stop loss too? Isn't the stop loss at the closing of the prices enough?"*

NO, because the market is unpredictable, because you never know what can happen, so without a protective stop loss **you risk at any time** that your account is drained by news or high volatility.

Let's see a real case:

Image 3.30: I identify supportive area on the silver charm and I set only the stop loss to the closing of the prices

We are on the daily chart of silver, through a technical study we realize to be in a downward trend because the maximums are decreasing, but we also notice a supportive area above which a doji is formed. The latter is formed slightly below the support, but it still remains an indication of indecision / reversal because the breakout of a level of very few pips can't be considered as a real breakout. In this situation some traders could decide to go upwards in order to take advantage of the retracement; personally, I would avoid it, as I would go against the trend, but as an entry it is not wrong.

Let's now imagine a trader who decides not to place the protective stop, but to use only the stop loss at the closing of prices, which is positioned below the level of 15,884 (conceding with the doji low). Our friend will close the position only if prices close at the end of the day below the 15,884 level.

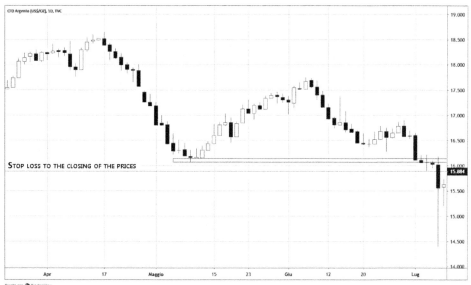

Image 3.31: Silver price collapse

After two days our friend is in position. The price of silver drops to a peak, and then closes at the end of the day new the level of 15,500. Our friend has therefore lost much more than 1% of its capital, approximately 3%, which is already too much for one position!

Let's imagine now that our friend during the day in which prices plummeted has opened his platform when silver marked 14.500, other than 1% of the capital, at that moment he is losing almost 15% of his capital, MADNESS!! From an emotional point of view our friend would have surely panicked and surely he would have acted in an irrational way with a good chance to worsen the already dramatic situation.

Through this silver example it is very easy to understand how to set both stops described in the chapter. Sure, cases like this one rarely occur in the markets, but whoever wants to make trading his job will surely find himself in front of such days and therefore he will have to be ready to defend his capital.

8: *Stop on break even after a profit*

The break-even stop after profit is one of the smartest things a trader can do when operating in the markets.

What do I mean with a breakeven stop after a profit?

I mean when you see that a position that you opened maybe a few days, or a few hours back - depending on the time frame you're using – that's in profit, but it hasn't taken your take profit yet, the BEST thing to do is ALWAYS to move the stop loss to break-even.

Why is this the best thing to do?

Because in case the market suddenly changes direction or it falls victim of high volatility you could turn a position that was bringing you profit into one that takes your stop loss. *There is no more irritating thing that can happen to a trader.* Thus, the best thing to do is to protect yourself from this situation: MOVE THE STOP LOSS TO THE BREAK EVEN.

This is not to say that as soon as your position starts gaining a few pips of profit you immediately set the breakeven stop, this could considerably reduce your chances of taking the potential gain that could bring you that operation. Of course the choice to move the stop has to be considered according to the situation.

There are two variables that must affect your choice of when to break even:

1) Market volatility: if you are operating in a very volatile market it will clearly make sense to move the stop to break even when you are in profit even if only by a few dimes and the chances of taking the stop due to a sudden swing of the instrument are low.

2) The time you want to keep the position open: the stop must always be related to this variable, for example if you decide to buy Facebook shares to keep them for a few years there is no point in putting the stop on even after two or three days, but it will make sense to do so only after a few months, when the stock will have appreciated.

The concept on which this trading commandment is based is basically the following: rather than losing, it is better to close the breakeven position.

Let me show you the following cases in which the break-even rule allowed me to safeguard my trading account and avoid losing money unnecessarily.

EUR/USD CASE

Image 3.32: I identify the trend and position stop loss to the closing of the prices and protective stop loss

This is the euro/dollar exchange rate on the 24 hour time frame. The first thing that should be noticed is that the trend is in a bearish phase characterized by decreasing highs and lows marked by the trend line. Here I realize that the prices in their descent have reached an important support in area 1.11934 and have created a hammer. At the closing of the candle, I decide to open a position to the rise, with stop loss at the closing of the prices under my support, stop loss protective to 1.11704, and target price the trend line superior. I would like to specify that I am well aware that what I am doing is an operation against trend, which is why my exposure will be distinctly inferior, at least half, compared to a position in favour of the main trend.

In the following days the prices start to move in the expected direction marking increasing highs and lows reaching area 1.3000 after eight sessions. At this point I realize that the prices are still far from my target price, but they are also far from my stop loss.

What does a good trader do in this situation?

A good trader at this point takes home half of the position and applies the first commandment, namely, he **MOVES THE STOP LOSS TO THE BREAK EVEN**, in our case in the 1.12148 area.

Image 3.33: I set the stop loss in even on the EUR/USD exchange rate

The advantages of this move are mainly 2:

1) If it goes wrong with this operation, the trader will not lose money.

2) The trader can sleep peacefully, i.e. he will no longer have to think: *uh my position on euro/dollar, who knows how the exchange rate is moving, hopefully I won't lose money...* and he will be able to focus on other trades, greatly reducing his stress level. This will lead him to be more lucid and calm and as a result more profitable.

What happens in the following days?

Image 3.34: The prices hit the stop loss in break-even

It happens that the dollar starts to appreciate against the euro and day after day it starts to eat away all the gain we made, until it drops below the 1.11934 level. But we are calm because we know that as far as the graph can go down we are covered because we moved the stop to breakeven.

The example shown above appears numerous times on the markets and many inexperienced traders are victims of it, thus suffering a great disappointment as well as a loss of money.

I recommend that when you use the strategy of the break-even stop do NOT EVER think: I *close the position now with little profit, because I have the breakeven stop...*

DO NOT DO IT!! If it hits the stop it closes as even otherwise, if it is not the case, let the position run. It is a matter of discipline, when trading you have to impose rules and always respect them, otherwise you become a victim of all those emotions that devour most traders who lose money.

SILVER CASE

With this second example I would like to show you how to go beyond the **breakeven stop** technique and start to use the **stop loss in profit**, to protect the gains gained through a trading operation.

Image 3.35: Trend analysis on the silver chart

We are on the silver graph on a daily time frame. From the image above what you can immediately notice is that the prices after a long sideways phase (which I have represented with a rectangle) have managed to break this important figure and have drawn two bullish candles. Here what a trader must observe and understand is that the silver prices after a long sideways phase started to rise, so the best thing to do is to look for price retracements and move in favour of the main trend.

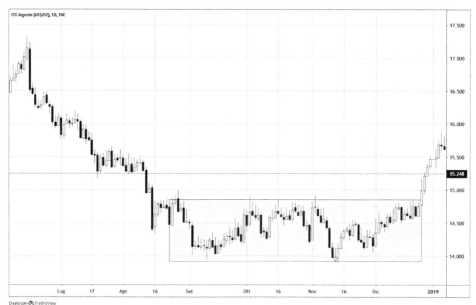

Image 3.36: I identify a potential upward support

In the following days we see how prices push upwards. At this point I notice the spinning top that informs me that the trend wants to slow down and we are going to prepare a retrace. In this case it is not necessary to enter short, because we would go against the main trend, but we look for a support to exploit to enter long. Searching in the past we discover that the prices had bounced more times on the level of 15.248, consequently I trace on my chart the support and I wait for the prices of silver to hit it to enter long. My targets in this operation are 15,800 first, then 16,200 and ultimately 17,000.

Image 3.37: I go upward on the silver and position stop loss at closing price and protective stop loss

The prices after some sessions finally reach the support in area 15.248, therefore I decide to enter long with stop to the closing of the prices under the level of 15.200 and stop loss protective 15.118. Remember, as I said in the point 7, that this stop must be chosen mainly according to the available capital. In the specific case of this operation I have decided, based on my exposure, to place it at 1% of my capital.

Image 3.38: I place the stop loss in even on silver

In the following days the prices rise sharply, therefore I apply the sixth law first; and then I take home a 1/3 of the position in area 15.800; and immediately afterwards I apply the eighth law, then I

TRANSFORM my protective Stop loss into the Stop loss in even, in area 15.307 so that even a sudden movement of the prices cannot catch me unprepared.

Image 3.39: I set the stop loss in profit on silver

After a few retracement sessions the prices of silver seem to be willing to start going upwards, but I'm not sure that my targets will be affected or that the previous highs, the shooting star in area 16,100, will be reached by prices. That's why I use the **STOP LOSS IN PROFIT**, this way I move the stop loss in even from the 15.307 area to the 15.479 area, which is just under the spinning top which has made the silver rise again. This way if the prices continue to rise I will reach my target, on the contrary I will not lose all the profit already gained.

Image 3.40: The prices hit the stop loss in profit

In the following days the prices rose strongly, they hit my second target in area 16.200, I applied the sixth law and achieved half of the position I have left, and then I let the last part of the position run, always keeping the stop loss in profit. In the following sessions the price of the silver begins to drop and the stop loss gets hit.

I want to highlight that if we had not applied the eighth law of the last third of our position, not only would we not have gained anything, but we would have lost money, as we would have had to close the loss-making position, because it would have hit the stop loss at the closing of prices as they went below the support in the 15,248 area.

9: *Stand still*

The ninth law is key for any type of trader you want to be: a scalper, an intraday trader, a swing trader, etc... and it is as follows: IF YOU DO NOT KNOW WHAT TO DO, **STAND STILL.**

Trading is not a quantity job like an employee in a company that is paid according to the number of hours they work, but a QUALITY job. In fact, it is not important how many trades a trader opens, it is fundamental WHAT he opens. I often see novice traders with a portfolio of 5 forex exchanges, 10 shares, 3 indexes and some crypto....

Does it look like an easy wallet to manage? The answer is NO, a portfolio that is too broad is very difficult to manage, especially for the less experienced ones.

Does it look like a successful portfolio? Possible... but you have to be very good, because all the correlations between the various financial instruments come into play and for a trader even with modest experience seeing the portfolio full of instruments creates confusion and **blurred judgment,** which is fundamental in trading, FUNDAMENTAL.

A job that reflects very much that of the trader is the painter. It is not important the amount of paintings he paints, but how he paints them. If the painter creates a work of art he earns enough money for 10 generations, and the same goes for the trader: if he buys the right shares at the right time and manages the position well he earns enough money for 10 generations. However, there is a difference between the painter and the trader: if the painter makes a mistake in the painting nothing happens, he just wastes time, but if a trader makes a mistake in the transaction it can be a disaster, because he loses money and money is the trader's raw material.

All this is to say that if a trader is not sure of the position he is about to open the best thing to do is to **STAND STILL**.

If you stand still you may lose an opportunity to make money, but you certainly suffer no losses.

Another scenario in which I recommend not to operate is when you are pressured for some reason, such as university exams, family problems, etc. In such situations you do not have full control of your emotionality, so you risk making trivial and serious mistakes such as opening positions of which you are not totally sure or widen the stop loss or even worse eliminate them to hope for some magical movement of the market. In short, trading allows us to earn well without having to work ten hours a day, but when you do it you have to be at the best of your mental capabilities, so that you can face the market in complete peace and security. If the day before you had an argument with your girlfriend or received bad news, turn off your computer, rest, do something else, relax, go to the pool, the sea, watch a movie just do not put yourself in front of the charts, because it exponentially increases your chances of becoming a victim of the market.

Another scenario where you do not have to operate in the market is when you suffer a series of consecutive losses. This rule is fundamental to safeguard your capital. When I trade and suffer a series of losses, I decide to turn off the pc and spend my time doing something else to avoid suffering further losses, perhaps even more serious.

The greatest risk that you run when you decide to trade on the market after a series of losses is to want to quickly recover the lost capital, maybe just to close the day or week in profit. The first thing that an inexperienced trader thinks, maybe three, four or five consecutive losses is: *I have already made a mistake five times, impossible that I make a mistake again... you know what? I expose myself a little more. I won't be wrong...* **GOOD JOB IDIOT,** this is exactly how you will burn your account. Never forget that the market doesn't give a damn about what we think, so we can make mistakes 100 times in a row, the important thing is never to lose control of the situation, and as soon as you realize that you are no longer mentally lucid you have to turn off the computer and enjoy life.

Another situation where it is better to stand still and not operate is definitely after important profits gained, perhaps in several consecutive positions, without ever finding even a loss. Now you may be wondering *why I should stand still if I'm in a great streak?* The answer is very simple, if you are in a very positive moment you will surely be very confident, you will feel like a dragon and you will start to believe that you have become a king of online trading. The biggest risk you will face is the excess of enthusiasm which could lead you to open numerous positions, even with high exposure, and in a very short time you could lose all the gain you have made with so much effort.

Another piece of advice that I feel like giving is to often take breaks from trading. As I mentioned before, our trade is a quality job so, when we feel tired, unmotivated and we put ourselves in front of the charts with little desire the best thing is to turn off the computer and take a break to rest your mind and be able to return after a few days to work with more energy.

The final case in which I strongly recommend to stand still is before the release of important news such as the change in interest rates, oil stocks, etc... Such news can significantly increase volatility within the market, creating confusion and stress for traders. By this I do not mean that if the US interest rate data comes out on Wednesday, we do not have to trade the whole week on the dollar, but only avoid entering the market on Wednesday. For open positions on the instrument that will be affected by the news, I recommend instead to protect yourself well with the stops discussed in the previous chapters and maybe if you are in profit collect a part of the position.

Summing up, there are six cases in which a trader must avoid trading:

- ➤ When you are not sure of the operation you are about to undertake
- ➤ When you are under pressure or particularly nervous
- ➤ After a consecutive series of losses
- ➤ After a consecutive series of closed trades in profit
- ➤ When you do not feel like trading
- ➤ Before the release of important economic data

10: *Do not trade alone*

Operating within the financial markets arouses great emotion in investors, who see second after second, changes in the capital they have made available for their investments, and the more this capital is substantial, the more important investments will be and, thus, the stronger the emotions will be. The secret of a successful trader is not in his knowledge of technical analysis - which however plays a fundamental role in the interpretation of financial markets - but in his skill to **be the absolute master of the emotions** and the capability of controlling them, regardless of what happens to his capital.

In trading, emotions swing between uncontrollable joy, fear, anger, discouragement and many others that I have already listed in the previous chapter. What I want to say is how to lighten all the emotional burden that trading brings. The secret is DO NOT TRADE ALONE.

Loneliness is one of the worst feelings that can be experienced, without analyzing all the psychological aspects that derive from this status, let's just say that IN TRADING LONELINESS IS LETHAL.

Why?

The reasons are mainly two:

- You can't share. *Share what?* Both positive and negative feelings, because there is no one to celebrate or rant with, who can really understand your mood.

- You cannot compare your analysis with other traders. In all things comparison is fundamental because it gives rise to ideas and dispels false myths allowing also some personal growth. The nice thing about trading is not in earning money from home, but in making analysis and sharing your own with others to learn, teach and improve.

How can you not be alone when trading?

The best thing to do is definitely to share this passion with a friend or family member. *What if none of my friends want to trade? What if there are two of us, but we have no experience?* My advice is to look for an online group of traders, maybe on some site. In Italy there are plenty of them. Personally the one I prefer and use, and where I also share my operations is tradingview.com. On this website you will find many traders with different levels of experience who share their operations and analysis.

Once you enter these groups you will feel much more confident because you will be able to routinely observe the workings of experienced traders, who will share their analysis, orders, stops and take profits with you. One recommendation that I would like to give you is to avoid turning into what I call a **LEECH TRADER.**

What is a leech trader?

The leech trader is a trader who discovers that copying the trades of his more experienced colleague improves his results, so he slowly decides to stop analyzing the markets, and all he does is watch videos and read articles from other traders to copy their trades. This, in the long term, is detrimental to the neophyte, who will never learn how to analyse the financial markets in the first place, and secondly, will have no idea how to manage the trade. That said I'm not saying you should never copy a trading operation, but before doing so I strongly suggest you to look for the instrument on your trading platform, analyse the chart, evaluate if your analysis coincides with the one you have read or seen, and only and exclusively if you realize that you are able to manage the operation, then you can operate. I also recommend you to be active in WhatsApp groups, websites, comments of other analysis, because only then you can put yourself on the line, evaluate your level of professionalism, learn from your mistakes and become a successful trader.

Lastly, I would like to remind you of the importance of being the masters of your trading business, because although it is a very difficult job that requires sacrifice, it pays off in the end, as it allows you to be **FREE**.

Now you are surely thinking: *but I am already free!* Free yes, you are not physically imprisoned, but your work imposes fixed schedules, precise obligations, duties and many, so much sacrifice, which very often benefit others. It is true that trading requires a lot of discipline, but if you want to rest one morning, you can do it, as we said in the previous chapter, it is not a work of quantity, but of quality. If one day you want to spend some quality time with your family you can do it and you don't have to ask permission from anyone. The most important thing is that with trading, the sacrifices you make, such as study hours, will be done for your benefit, and everything you learn won't be taken away from you.

Should I then quit my job to trade?

If you don't like your job and go to work unwillingly, for a measly salary, just waiting for retirement, the answer is ABSOLUTELY YES.

Of course, you don't have to abruptly leave your job, but you have to dedicate yourself to trading slowly, for a few **YEARS**, in parallel with your work, and only when you start to be an expert can you get rid of a job that does not satisfy you and that limits your potential.

The last piece of advice I would like to give you is to believe in yourself that you really want to become a professional trader and not to give up when you have to face challenges. In fact, as Peter Lynch, famous stock investor, says: *"Everyone has the mental capacity to invest in the stock market. But not everyone has enough will and guts".*

THE 10 LAWS TO CONTROL THE MARKET

Rewrite this page and paste it next to the monitor, so that you always remember how to have full control of the market and your operations.

1: Always follow the main trend

2: Earn more than you lose

3: Supports and resistances are price ranges

4: Work easy, few indicators

5: Do not anticipate the market

6: Split the position

7: Stop loss at candle closure and protective stop loss

8: Stop on break even after a profit

9: Stand still

10: Do not trade alone

Chapter 4

Trading marketing

4.1 Trading diffusion thanks to marketing

Until the end of the nineties most of the investments on the financial markets were made mainly by the big investment banks, while private investors represented a very small share in the world financial landscape. The only possibility of opening buying or selling positions was to call one's broker or bank by phone, so the convenience of this mechanism was minimal and did not allow trading to spread. Among the main problems, it is important to note:

- The difficulty of finding prices in real time, as a result, the few operators on the markets never knew exactly what price the financial instrument was at that precise moment.
- No technical analysis tools, such as specific indicators or charts, were available, so the only criterion by which the securities were bought and sold was the news that could be found in financial newspapers.
- The delay with which a purchase or sale transaction was confirmed to the customer by the bank. This problem made it impossible to operate in the financial markets with day trading or scalping strategies.

Nowadays, thanks to numerous factors, the influence of the banks on the markets has been significantly reduced and the influence of small private investors who can operate on the financial markets with a capital of a few hundred euros has increased exponentially.

This diffusion of online trading among small investors has not been immediate; in fact it has increased thanks to the marketing strategies adopted by large international brokers to increase their clients. These strategies are based on making people believe that with online trading you can get rich quickly with just a few clicks. Whereas, to be successful in the financial markets and earn money, you need to start an in-depth study, along with commitment and dedication. However, the goal of big brokers has been achieved, leading to an unprecedented increase in the number of traders in the markets. This has caused an increase in volatility in the financial markets because the presence of more investors has led to more transactions and these have caused more movements in the markets.

As far as the broker market is concerned, it is very competitive in fact only in Italy in 2017 it was recorded the presence of 132 online brokers authorized by Corncob, compared to 120 in 2016 and 118 in 2015.

In order to increase its clients, the various trading platforms rely on the following marketing strategies:

- Online advertising: it allows you to reach the general public who surfs the internet; and it allows the viewer to immediately understand how online trading works.

- Sponsors: Major online brokers hold partnership contracts with major football clubs in order to put their brand on the players' shirts. It is no coincidence that soccer has been chosen as the most popular sport in the world, allowing it to reach as many users as possible.

- Business phone calls: Use once the most curious people have registered on the platform to immediately create a bond with the customer and provide them with the main instructions to open a real account.

- Welcome bonus: Some brokers to increase the interest of the public offer a welcome bonus ranging between 25 and 50 euros to new users who have completed the registration. This practice was used until 2017, after which time some international regulations were issued so it is no longer possible for platforms to offer this service.

- Consulting services: These are provided only by a few brokers and consist of an exchange of information between platform operators and small investors. This service may seem practical, in fact for a novice trader it is even harmful, because only he knows his risk appetite and financial level. Moreover, relying on the advice of other individuals, the small investor will not be able to create his own operational strategy and consequently will never enrich his knowledge.

The use of such strategies shows important results in the online broker market, even if the high competitiveness present is leading the various platforms to increasingly aggressive marketing techniques, which risk creating in the public mind the idea that online trading is just a tool to take money from people, comparing it more and more to casino gambling.

4.2 Leverage

One of the reasons that allowed trading to spread quickly and create in the minds of traders the idea of a tool to get rich quickly is certainly leverage. It can be defined both as a tool to improve your operations in the markets and as a marketing strategy. Given the effects it generates, I think it is more appropriate to include it in this chapter rather than the previous ones.

Through leverage it is possible to invest very large amounts of money with reduced capital in your account. Let's take as an example a trading platform offering 1:30 leverage and a trader with a capital of only 1000 euros, in case there is no leverage if all 1000 euros are invested and there is a 1% change in the market, then the profit for the trader would be 10 euros. If, on the other hand, the 1:30 leverage is applied and the trader decides to invest all 1000 euros, and there is a 1% change in the market, then the profit for the trader would be 300 euros, because investing this amount with a 1:30 leverage is as if he had committed 30,000 euros. It is important to emphasize that there are various types of financial levers, which depend both on the type of broker and the traded instrument, which are usually very high in the forex, commodities and indices market, while they are relatively low in the stock market. They range from a 1:1 lever up to 1:30 levers, normally intermediate financial levers are used always taking into account the economic availability of the investor and his propensity to risk. Until July 2018, the maximum leverage that could be used on certain financial instruments was 1:300, but was reduced following the entry into force of certain regulations imposed by ESMA

(European Securities and Markets Authority). Ultimately, it is worth emphasizing that leverage is a double-edged sword, in fact although it is able to increase profits it can at the same time and proportionally increase losses. Referring to the previous example, if the market had recorded a loss of 1% and the trader had invested his 1000 euros with a 1:30 leverage, he would have suffered a loss of 300 euros, leading him to dramatically reduce his trading account. For this reason it is advisable to be very careful and cautious in the choice of leverage because it can bring both great satisfaction and major disappointments at the same time.

4.3 New technologies in the technical analysis field

The great diffusion of financial trading has not only happened through marketing strategies, but also thanks to the interaction of these with the new technologies that have emerged in the last twenty years. First of all, it is worth stressing out that the spread of the Internet has allowed great mobility in the exchange of information and has speeded up transactions within the markets, thus allowing operators to make use of day trading and scalping strategies.

Secondly, the development of online platforms has solved the problem of finding prices in real time, allowing the construction of immediate charts ready to be analysed by potential investors. Thirdly, the possibility of opening a trading account in just a few minutes has been created via the internet, thus fuelling the process of spreading the phenomenon. Finally, thanks to the continuous innovation of trading platforms, it is possible to quickly create indicators and oscillators which, if they were to be created manually, would steal hours of work from analysts.

All these innovations have contributed to the worldwide phenomenon called online trading which is going through the most golden and profitable period of its history.

Chapter 5
Real cases

Below I will show you some real cases in which I will apply the 10 rules to control the market, so as to show you how, through the use of these precautions, you can always have control of what happens in the markets.

Intesa San Paolo case

Let's make an analysis on the Intesa San Paolo stock

Image 5.1: Analysis of the trend and identification of the supportive area of the Stock Intesa San Paolo

From the daily chart we can see that prices after dropping considerably throughout the month of May, they bounced for the first fortnight of June, on an important supportive area, around the 1.8125 level. From here they started to rise. Through these considerations I decide to highlight all the support in question and I wait for prices to return to that level to understand how they will behave.

Personally I expect a break in support, because prices are derived from a bearish trend, but I don't want to leave prejudiced as seen in the course of the book: "prices don't care about what I think".

Image 5.2: Position entry and target definition

Between the 12th and 13th of August the prices are finally back to my supportive area and once they hit it, they start with force upwards drawing a high volume candle, which informs me that the support has fully worked. Seeing as it has behaved the title to close of my support I decide to the end of the day, therefore approximately a quarter of hour before that the market closes, to enter long with stop loss to the closing of the prices under the low side of my rectangle and stop loss protective to the 1.7800 level, this last one coincides with one percent of my capital.

My targets are the previous supports encountered by the prices that have now become resistances, specifically the levels are: 1.990, 2.0645 and 2.1190.

Image 5.3: Prices hit my first target

In the following days the stock takes strength and the prices reach my first target, at this point I close 35% of my position and I move the stop break even stop loss, then to the 1.8885 level, so as to protect myself in case of sudden drops.

Image 5.4: Prices rise sharply and reach all targets set

Towards the beginning of September prices reached my second target, so I closed a further 35% of my position, remaining on the market with only 30% of the position I had initially opened. After just two days the stock reaches the level of 2,1190, so I close an additional 25% of my position. In this case I decide to leave a 5% of the position open for the long term because I believe in the company I invested in, but I still keep the breakeven stop loss.

SPX500 Case

Let us now analyse a real case of the most important index in the world, namely SPX500.

Image 5.5: Trend analysis and bullish engulfing on the SPX500 Index

We are on the daily chart of the index, at a first glance we immediately realize that we are in a bearish trend as there are decreasing highs and lows. This trend however gives the idea of being able to stop when at the end of December the prices create an important bullish candle that came along the previous one form an important pattern of reversal that is the engulfing line.

Image 5.6: Definition of a resistance area on the SPX500 Index

In the following days prices start to rise, but the trend change that I am waiting for has not yet been defined, so I identify the most important resistance, which is between $2620 and $2630. According to how the prices will behave on this level I will decide if to enter the rise or to estimate a short, not knowing it but I do not make useless suppositions, simply I wait and I look.

Image 5.7: Upward entry on SPX500 and definition of stops and targets

After a few sessions the prices break my area of upward resistance, it was already possible to enter upward at the closing of the breakout candle, but personally I prefer to wait for the retracement on the new support, that is the resistance that has been broken, which occurs after a couple of days and where the prices draw a candle of indecision/reversion. Consequently to the closing of the doji I decide to enter the rise with protective stop loss to the level of 2580$ (1% of my capital) and stop loss to the closing of the prices below the lower side of the rectangle, which coincides with the minimum of the doji. My targets are 2815$ in first and then 2937$.

Image 5.8: Prices reach the set targets

In the following months the prices continue to rise and hit my first target in area 2815$, once reached I decide to transform my protective stop loss in a break even stop loss, also close 60% of my position, as I have only two targets and I'm already positioned in the market for a long time. I will therefore run the remaining 40% which reaches my final target after about two months.

GBP/AUD case

Let's analyse a GBP/AUD exchange rate transaction

Image 5.9: Formation of a descending triangle on the GBP/AUD exchange rate

From the daily chart we notice that prices are within a descending triangle composed of the bearish trend line and the supportive area around the 1.81300 level. Considering this situation I prefer to wait to understand how prices will behave, that is if they will break the downward support, or the upward trend line.

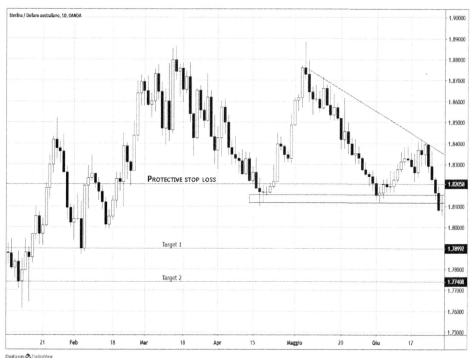

Image 5.10: Position entry on GBP/AUD exchange rate and stop and target definition

After a couple of days the prices break downwards in my supportive area and the following day also the retracement on the support takes place, so at the closing of the doji I decide to enter short on the gearbox. The protective stop loss I place it at 1.82058, while the stop loss at the closing of the prices is above the upper side of the rectangle. I find my targets by zooming in the chart and looking for old supports that have worked in the past, in this case I identify the 1.78992 level as first target and 1.7748 as second target.

Image 5.11: Prices reach the set targets

After only 3 trading days the prices reach my first target and therefore I close 60% of my position and let the remaining 40% run to my final target, which is reached after approximately ten days. But what I would like to focus on is the July 1st candle, highlighted by the ellipse. When it was drawn the candle in question I was already positioned down on the exchange rate, as I entered at the closing of the doji, this means that on the first of July I suffered on my position, in fact the closing prices were very close to my stop loss at the closing of prices. In this case someone could think: *tomorrow it will take it for sure, I'll go out now.* Luckily I did not think in this way, because I use a very precise strategy and I respect it with the necessary discipline, which is essential to be a successful trader.

In trading, errors, losses and failure are the standard, they happen all the time with a scary regularity.

The strongest weapon that a person who wants to become a profitable trader possesses is perseverance, because only when you give up have you really lost.

Nothing in this world can replace perseverance: neither talent, cunning nor education.

Only perseverance and determination are omnipotent, proving that nothing will ever defeat you, that you can achieve your goals, better health and an unceasing flow of energy.

References

- Fanton S., *Lo zen la via del trader samurai*, Milano, Traderpedia book, 2016.
- Hagstrom R., *Il metodo Warren Buffet,* Milano, Hoelpli, 2014.
- Morris G., *Manuale di analisi candlestick*, Milano, Trading library, 2007.
- Murphy J., *Analisi tecnica dei mercati finanziari*, Milano, Hoelpli, 2002.
- Numerosi autori, *I consigli dei grandi trader*, Milano, Hoepli, 2016.
- Probo G., *La mente del trader*, Milano, Hoepli, 2014.
- Probo G., *Trading di profitto*, Milano, Hoepli, 2017.
- Probo G., *Trading operativo sul forex*, Milano, Hoepli, 2012.
- Weisz S., *Il day trading nel forex*, Milano, BookSprintEdizioni, 2014.

Printed in Great Britain
by Amazon